INVADERS
OF SCOTLAND

ANNA RITCHIE AND DAVID J. BREEZE

INVADERS
OF SCOTLAND

AN INTRODUCTION TO THE ARCHAEOLOGY
OF THE ROMANS, SCOTS, ANGLES AND VIKINGS,
HIGHLIGHTING THE MONUMENTS IN THE CARE OF
THE SCOTTISH MINISTERS

Society is a partnership
not only between those who are living
but between those who are living,
those who are dead,
and those who are to be born.

Edmund Burke (1729-97)

HISTORIC SCOTLAND

EDINBURGH: HISTORIC SCOTLAND

Inside front cover
This sculpture of a lioness was found in the bed of the River Almond at Cramond in 1996. In her jaws the lioness holds a man by his head. The sculpture, which is not made from local stone, may have come from a funerary monument. The fort at Cramond was occupied by the Romans in the second and early third centuries: some of its buildings may be seen in the park beside the kirk.

frontispiece
The bath-house at **Bearsden** on the Antonine Wall looking from the changing room towards the heated ranges. This is the best-preserved Roman stone building visible in Scotland.

Opposite
Jarlshof, Shetland. Beyond the medieval laird's house rise the precipitous cliffs of Sumburgh Head.

Back cover
The head of a goddess, probably Fortuna, found in the Roman bath-house at **Bearsden**. Fortuna protected men from the evil eye when they were in their most vulnerable state, naked.

Crown Copyright ©
Historic Scotland 2000

ISBN 1 900168 77 4

CONTENTS

Note: Those monuments in State care mentioned in the book are shown in **bold** type. Reference to other sites does not imply that they are accessible to the public.

THE CANVAS PREPARED

This sculpture of three Roman legionaries found at **Croy Hill** is probably part of a tombstone, perhaps a father and his two sons.

Between the Roman military invasion of AD 79 and the peaceful Normandy "invasion by invitation" during the 12th century the canvas of Scotland's population was worked with threads of many colours. These were centuries of political change throughout Europe, and Scotland was relatively stable compared to other areas; nevertheless, a succession of invaders brought new blood to the population and new ideas to alter its lifestyle. The main chapters in this book will explore the contributions made by the Romans, the Scots (or Gaels), the Angles and the Vikings to an indigenous canvas of Britons and Picts. All these various peoples have left archaeological traces of their forts, houses, burials and stone-carving, and many of the most interesting sites to visit are in State care.

The Celtic world that the Romans encountered belongs to prehistory, and its interpretation is the work of the archaeologist. The landscape of the 1st century AD was dominated by the strongholds of a Celtic tribal society: the forts, duns and brochs described in a companion volume in this series, Scotland BC. The wealth and livelihood of these tribes was founded on stock-rearing and agriculture, and it is likely that the Roman army derived some of its supplies of grain and meat locally from the farms and villages of southern and eastern Scotland. A side-effect of the Roman invasion was to give us the names of these tribes and even some placenames – a luxury normally denied to the archaeologist working on prehistoric material. Using information gathered on military expeditions, the Greek geographer Ptolemy,

The earthwork defences of **Ardoch** Roman fort. Five ditches survive on the east side, seen here.

Opposite
Against the backdrop of industrial Clydeside, the British stronghold of **Dumbarton Rock** still dominates the seaway. No trace of the early fort is visible, and the succeeding medieval castle was replaced by later defences, including the Governor's House of 1735.

Dragon or lion, this vigorous carving in **Maes Howe**, Orkney, is part of Scotland's Viking heritage.

working in Alexandria in the 2nd century AD, included on his map of the world the names of 16 tribes in the area that we now call Scotland, along with some names of settlements, rivers and other geographical features. Remarkably his treatise, simply called *Geography*, has survived the intervening centuries. Beyond the River Tay lived the Caledonian tribes who, by AD 297, had joined together to form the Picts (the subject of another volume in this series, Picts).

The tribes with whom the Romans would probably have had most contact were the Votadini of south-east Scotland, the Selgovae of central southern Scotland, the Novantae of the south-west, the Damnonii of the Strathclyde area and the Vanicones of Fife. South of the Forth-Clyde line, these were the native British peoples who by the 6th century had created the kingdoms of Gododdin in the Lothian area (with a stronghold on **Castle Rock, Edinburgh**), Strathclyde (with a stronghold on **Dumbarton Rock**) and Rheged in south-west Scotland (one of whose strongholds was probably Mote of Mark in Kirkcudbrightshire).

These three British kingdoms were forced in the 7th century to contend with aggression from their neighbours to the south-east – the Angles, a Germanic people originally from Schleswig-Holstein (or Angeln), who were by then firmly established in the north-eastern part of the country that was later named after them, England.

Dunadd in Argyll was an important Scottish stronghold.

By the mid-6th century there were two Anglian kingdoms in north Britain: Bernicia with its royal stronghold at Bamburgh, and Deira based at York. Tension between Briton and Angle developed into outright warfare. If King Arthur may be seen as more than literary invention, it is to this period, around AD 500, that he and the power struggles that he represents belong.

The history of both Northumbria and Pictland begins in the mid-6th century with their respective kings, Ida of Bernicia and Bridei son of Maelchon of Pictland, and the Picts were to suffer in the 7th century at Anglian hands just as their fellow Britons. In the long term, however, the Angles failed to penetrate permanently beyond the Firth of Forth.

In the meantime, a new Scottish kingdom of Dalriada had been founded around AD 500 in Argyll, as a result of settlers migrating from Northern Ireland. The political histories of Dalriada and Pictland became increasingly closely interwoven over the next three centuries, until, around 843, the two kingdoms were united and Pictland became Scotland. One factor that contributed to this fusion was the presence of Viking raiders and settlers along the Atlantic coasts, and this colourful Scandinavian thread was to become an essential part of the canvas of early medieval Scotland.

One more thread remains to be mentioned, one that runs through and unites all the others: Christianity. The initial introduction of Christianity to Scotland is credited to two major figures and their missionary followers: St Ninian, based at **Whithorn** in Galloway in the 5th century, to whom the evangelisation of southern Scotland is credited, and St Columba, based on Iona in the 6th century, who introduced Christianity to the Picts and whose followers founded monasteries both in Pictland and in Northumbria. Southern Scotland boasts some of the earliest and finest Christian memorial stones, including those at **Whithorn** itself (see p 35) and at **Kirkmadrine** in the Rhins of Galloway. These early incised carvings are matched by the symbol stones of the Picts, but the full glory of the sculptor's achievement comes with the cross-slabs and free-standing crosses commissioned by princes, noblemen and the Church in the 8th to 10th centuries, whether Pictish, Scottish or Northumbrian.

The first thousand years after the birth of Christ were, in Scotland, as elsewhere in western Europe, an exciting time of change. Scotland is fortunate in having a wide range of visible monuments surviving from this period, from the forts, camps, watch-towers and roads of Roman times to the strongholds, settlements, monasteries and sculpture of Scots, Angles and Vikings – the invaders of early historic Scotland.

Iona, the Christian heart of Scottish Dalriada, whose influence was far-ranging in early medieval times.

Tonsured clerics make a purposeful pair on this cross-slab in the collection at **St Vigeans**, Angus.

4

AN ARMY ON THE MOVE– THE ROMANS INVADE SCOTLAND

Two Roman cavalrymen ride out: a scene on Trajan's Column in Rome.

The Emperor Domitian, who appears on this coin, ordered the invasion of northern Scotland in AD 82. This coin was issued in AD 86. Within two years all army units appear to have been withdrawn from Scotland north of the Tay.

I N AD 79 the Roman army under Gnaeus Julius Agricola, governor of Britain, reached the River Tay. Four years later the same army defeated the Caledonian tribes at the battle of Mons Graupius and the conquest of Britain seemed to be assured. But this was not to be. Within a generation the Romans had withdrawn to the Tyne-Solway line, where they were to build Hadrian's Wall in the 120s; and for the next 300 years that Wall was to be the north-west frontier of the Roman empire. On two occasions, in the 140s and again from 208 to 211, Roman armies conquered southern Scotland, and in the 4th century there were also to be military expeditions against the Picts; but for most of that period the Roman influence in Scotland was restricted to the occupation of outpost forts in the Cheviots and its foothills, to the mounting of scouting patrols, and the formalising of treaties with its Celtic tribal chieftains. Northern Scotland remained unconquered, and southern Scotland was frontier country.

The Invasion of Scotland

The Romans invaded Britain in AD 43 not for economic reasons but, according to the Roman writer Suetonius, in order to provide the new emperor, Claudius, with military prestige. In a military dictatorship such as the Roman Empire the winning of military victories was the best way for an emperor to secure his position on the throne. Claudius duly gained his triumph and promptly lost interest in Britain. It was the accession of a new emperor, Vespasian, in 69 that brought about a change in policy. Vespasian had served in the army of invasion. He ordered a new

Tacitus records that Agricola pressed forward his invasion of Caledonia by land and by sea. On this scene on Trajan's Column, erected in AD 113, tents are being loaded on to a ship.

Opposite
The Antonine Wall ditch at **Watling Lodge** survives close to its original dimensions, 12 m wide and about 4 m deep. The ditch is the most enduring feature of this north-west frontier of the Roman Empire.

5

This section across the Antonine Wall was excavated by Professor Anne Robertson in 1959. The rampart stands nearly 1.5 m (5 feet) high. The black lines caused by the rotted turf are clearly visible, as is the stone base.

Below left
A reconstruction of the watch-tower on the Gask Ridge at **Muir O' Fauld** by M J Moore. The timber tower sits within a rampart and ditch. Towers like these lay along the road north from the Forth to the Tay. They appear to date to the late 1st century. (The much-denuded earthworks of a second tower are in State care at **Ardunie**.)

Below right
The Antonine Wall running over **Croy Hill** looking west towards **Bar Hill**. The ditch is clearly visible in the foreground. The rampart has long since been ploughed flat, but the upcast mound to the right (north) survives well. The line of the Wall is continued at the top of the picture as a field boundary.

initiative in Britain and within the space of less than 15 years his governors conquered northern England, Wales and southern Scotland.

Gnaeus Julius Agricola came to Britain as governor in AD 77. After operations elsewhere he moved north in 79, reaching the River Tay. The tribes of southern Scotland were incorporated into the province, the Forth-Clyde isthmus was garrisoned, and there the Roman advance halted. Agricola turned his attention to other matters, campaigning in the west and even toying with the idea of an invasion of Ireland. In 82 he returned to this northern advance, moving against the tribes of Caledonia. It was not until nearly the end of the following season that he was able to force – and win – a set-piece battle at an unknown location called Mons Graupius. It was an 18th-century misreading of this name which led the Grampian mountains to be so named.

Agricola had served in Britain for seven campaigns and he retired soon after his victory. He clearly considered that he had decisively defeated the Caledonians, and his son-in-law, the Roman historian Tacitus, was to write, about 15 years later, that Britain was conquered. Roman success was short-lived. Heavy military defeats on the Danube forced the Romans to withdraw part of their army from Britain in 87 or 88, and as a result most forts beyond the Cheviots were abandoned. By the end of the century those bases in turn were given up and the most northerly Roman forts lay on the Tyne-Solway isthmus. The status quo was recognised by the Emperor Hadrian, who ordered the construction of his Wall on that line.

Hadrian's Wall took many years to build. Work probably started in 122 or 123 and the troops were still modifying the frontier installations at the time of the emperor's death in 138. Within a few months his successor, Antoninus Pius, decided on a new forward policy in Britain and preparations started in 139 with the recommissioning of the fort at Corbridge on one of the two main routes into Scotland.

The Antonine Wall
The reconquest of southern Scotland was completed by AD 142 and work began on the military installations designed to ensure the Roman grip on the area. A new frontier, the **Antonine Wall**, was built across the narrow waist of Scotland, the Forth-Clyde isthmus. Behind the Wall regiments were based in the forts and fortlets on the roads leading north. Hadrian's Wall was abandoned, together with most of the forts to its south.

At 40 Roman miles (= 37 statute miles or nearly 60 km) long, the Antonine Wall was just half the length of Hadrian's Wall. It consisted of a turf rampart, perhaps 3 m high, placed on a stone base probably intended to be 15 Roman feet (= 4.3 m) wide. In front lay a wide and deep ditch. The material from the ditch was tipped out on to the north side to form an outer mound. Along the Wall lay forts, fortlets and 'expansions', which were perhaps beacon-platforms. The first plan entailed the construction of six forts along the Wall with a fortlet at each mile interval in between. Before this scheme was completed the decision was made to add at least ten more forts to

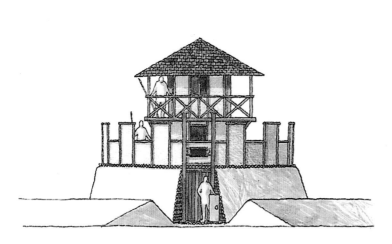

the Wall, reducing the distance between each from about 8 miles to a little over 2 miles.

These forts held either whole regiments or smaller detachments. The 6,000 men based in these forts were not there to defend the Wall itself, but to protect the province from attack. In the event of a major invasion they would move out into the field to meet the enemy in a set-piece battle, at which the Roman army was pre-eminent. The purpose of the **Antonine Wall** was essentially bureaucratic. It

The stone base of the rampart in New Kilpatrick Cemetery, Bearsden.

A reconstruction of the **Antonine Wall** by M J Moore. The fortlet guards a crossing point through the Wall. Accommodation for the soldiers is provided by the two buildings. To the right is an 'expansion', here interpreted as a beacon-platform for signalling. The remains of a fortlet can be seen at Kinneil near Bo'ness.

Left
The successful reconquest of southern Scotland in the late 140s was recorded on the coinage of the Emperor Antoninus Pius. This coin was issued in 144 and shows the emperor on one side and Britannia on the reverse.

Below
The distance slab found at Bridgeness near the east end of the Antonine Wall records the construction of 4^2/$_3$ miles of the wall by soldiers of Legion II Augusta. To the left a soldier rides down a group of four barbarians, while to the right a sacrifice is celebrated.

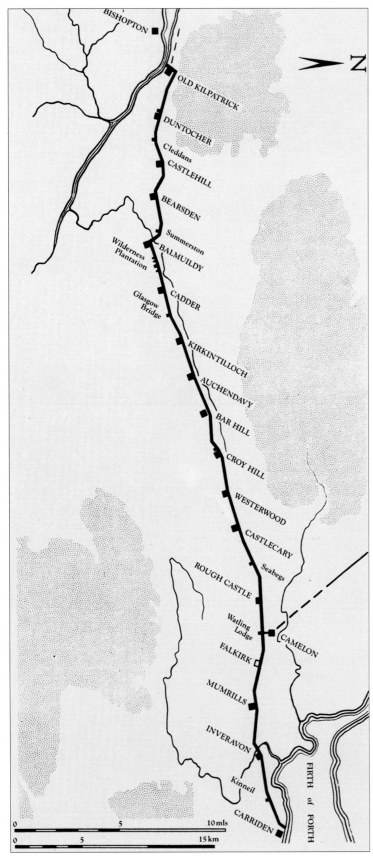

was to mark the difference between Roman and barbarian territory, prevent unauthorised entry to the empire and enforce the regulations which governed access to the guarded entrances (forts and fortlets). The new Wall was built in the most convenient geographical location, but it was not necessarily the frontier of the empire, for three or four outpost forts lay to the north.

The outline of the reconquest of southern Scotland at this time is clear; the reasons are less so. Various suggestions have been made: an enigmatic reference by a Greek travel writer offers the possibility that warfare north of Hadrian's Wall led to the northern advance; perhaps Hadrian's Wall had been built too far south to deal effectively with the main threat in the north, the Caledones of northern Scotland; the Romans wished to take direct control of the good agricultural land of the Lothians; the new emperor, Antoninus Pius, required military prestige and chose Britain as a place to gain that, just as his predecessor Claudius had done nearly 100 years before. The truth will never be known, but it is likely that the Romans could have dealt with any military threat by force without the need for the construction of a new Wall and all its ancillary works. The obtaining of military prestige through a foreign adventure may not be as far-fetched as it first seems: such actions are not unknown today.

The new frontier arrangements do not seem to have long outlasted the death of their initiator. Antoninus Pius died in 161, and the **Antonine Wall** and its attendant forts appear to have been abandoned about this time. The army returned to Hadrian's Wall, which was recommissioned. The system of control now established over the Scottish Lowlands was to last, with some modifications, for 200 years. At first, outpost forts were held as far north as Newstead on the River Tweed in the east and Birrens in the west. Before the end of the century these were reduced to four in number, two in the west and two in the east. These were the bases for both regular units and, in all probability, also scouts. These soldiers will have ranged widely in their patrols, perhaps over the whole of the former provincial territory. Also, by the end of the century treaties existed with the two main tribes living beyond the **Antonine Wall**, the Maeatae and the Caledones. These treaties may have been supported by gifts, including cash, to the local chiefs.

The Antonine Wall.

The Severan Invasion

The last years of the 2nd century were not peaceful on the northern frontier in spite of these arrangements. About AD 180, so Cassius Dio tells us, 'the tribes in the island crossed the wall that separated them from the Roman forts, did a great deal of damage, and cut down a general and his troops'. The emperor responded by sending a new governor to the island, and a Roman victory was achieved. Towards the end of the century, civil war erupted in the empire, and when peace was restored a new governor was sent to Britain. He found the northern frontier in a disturbed state. 'The Caledonians', wrote Cassius Dio, 'instead of honouring their promises, prepared to assist the Maeatae', and the new governor 'had to purchase peace from the Maeatae for a great sum, recovering a few prisoners'. Ten years later the army was recorded winning wars in Britain, yet in 208 the emperor himself determined to come to Britain in order to complete the conquest of the island. The immediate reasons was that the governor of Britain had written to report that the situation had deteriorated and that either more

troops or the presence of the emperor was required. The Emperor Septimius Severus decided to respond positively to both requests. He brought a large army to Britain, and also his two sons, Caracalla and Geta. Two contemporary historians, Cassius Dio and Herodian, record the reasons offered for this British expedition: the emperor wished to remove his sons from the decadent atmosphere of Rome and give them some military experience; the army required stiffening through combat; the emperor himself enjoyed campaigning; and there was trouble on the northern frontier.

Campaigning probably began in AD 209. After some hard fighting, mainly guerrilla warfare on the part of the local tribes, the Roman army forced their submission. In 210, however, they rose in rebellion and, as Severus was now too ill to campaign himself, he sent his son Caracalla to lead the Roman army, charged with orders to kill everyone that it met – the normal Roman treatment of rebels. Severus died at York on

A glass bottle, probably manufactured in the 2nd century, and found at Turiff in Aberdeen.

Coin of the Emperor Septimius Severus who came to Britain in 208 intending to complete the conquest of the island. The coin records his victory: *VICT BRIT.*

This hoard of nearly 2000 silver denarii was buried at Falkirk near the abandoned Antonine Wall in or soon after 235. The hoard may have been formed from subsidies paid by the Romans to local chiefs.

Five objects from the late 4th- or early 5th-century treasure found at Traprain Law in East Lothian. The treasure was probably either booty from the continent, or part of a subsidy paid by Rome to the local tribe, the Votadini.

Below right
A fragment of a monumental building inscription found in front of the east gate of the legionary base at Carpow on the south shore of the Tay estuary. The figures are the goddess Victory and two military symbols, the capricorn and the pegasis. These are the symbols of Legion II Augusta, which was based at Caerleon in South Wales. Their appearance on the building inscription demonstrates that soldiers of this legion came to Scotland to build the fort at Carpow. This base is the only fort known to have been built by the Emperor Septimius Severus in Scotland.

This fragment of a Roman altar was found in 1922 at **Jedburgh Abbey**. It reads: *Coh(ors) I Fid(a) Vardul(lorum) c(ivium) R(omanorum) m(illiaria) eq(uitata) et G(aius) Quintius Severus trib(unus) coh(ortis) eiusdem dom(o) Camil(ia tribu) Ravenna v(otum) s(olvern) l(ibens) m(erito)* (The First Loyal Cohort of Vardullians, a thousand strong, part-mounted, and Gaius Quintius Severus, tribune of the same cohort, of the Camilian voting tribe from Ravenna, gladly, willingly and deservedly fulfilled their vow). This regiment was based at High Rochester, across the Cheviots, in the early 3rd century.

4 February 211, possibly before the uprising had been quashed. Caracalla abandoned his father's conquests and withdrew Roman troops from the newly constructed forts, hastening to Rome, the centre of power. The northern tribes had been saved from incorporation into the Roman empire.

The Rise of the Picts
This was to be the last major Roman incursion into Scotland. Hadrian's Wall became once again the north-west frontier of the Roman empire. The location of four outpost forts to the north are known, Bewcastle and Netherby in Cumbria and Risingham and High Rochester in Northumberland. To the north of this last site, however, there was probably another base near Jedburgh where two inscriptions, probably dating to the early 3rd century, have been found. They point to a continuing Roman presence in southern Scotland.

The 3rd century appears to have been a time of peace, and no trouble is recorded on the northern frontier, though that may merely be a reflection of our poor sources. But in 297 a Roman writer refers for the first time to a new nation in the north, the Picts. Roman armies were to meet the Picts (the descendants of the Caledonians and their allies) on several occasions in the 4th century. In 306, the Emperor Constantius Chlorus campaigned against them shortly before his death. His more famous son, Constantine the Great, may have followed in his father's footsteps eight years later. Constantine's son, Constans, came to Britain in the winter of 342-3, possibly to deal with a disturbance in the north. In 360 the Emperor Julian sent a field army to restore order, and in 367, following a major invasion by the Picts, Scots and their allies, order could only be restored by the dispatch of a sizeable force from the continent. There was another invasion in 384, repulsed by the Romans, and one apparently at the very end of that century. The situation had by now been turned round. The earlier invaders were now being attacked by the descendants of the people whom they had set out to conquer.

The Roman Army

The Roman army which had taken part in the earlier campaigns was one of the most successful fighting forces that the world has ever seen. For nearly eight centuries it was pre-eminent in the field. The core of that fighting force until the late 3rd century was the legion. There were about 30 legions in the empire, each a little over 5,000 strong. Four were stationed in Britain until AD 87 or 88, when one was withdrawn. These heavily armed infantry regiments were supported by smaller units, nominally either 500 or 1,000 strong, either infantry or cavalry, or a mixture of both. In the 2nd century there were over 60 such units in Britain, giving a total strength for the army of the province of about 53,000. Not all these soldiers were based on the northern frontier. There may have been 30,000 men in the north, bearing in mind that not all units would have been at full strength.

These regiments were based in forts. Generally these forts, linked by roads, were about a day's march (some 14 - 20 miles) apart, though they were closer on the frontiers such as Hadrian's Wall and the **Antonine Wall**. The barrack-blocks for the soldiers were normally built of timber. In the 1st century the commanding officer's house, the headquarters building and the granaries were also of timber, but in the 2nd century they were usually of stone. The buildings were packed together relatively tightly and were surrounded by ramparts of turf (stone was rarely used) and at least two ditches. Up to four gates provided for easy movement.

The forts – and frontiers – were built by the soldiers themselves. Each legion contained its own architect-engineers, surveyors, masons and carpenters; even a glazier is attested. There is no evidence that the army received any outside help in its construction projects, though there is a possibility that civilians were used in the fetching and carrying of materials.

The use of turf to build the fort ramparts – and the **Antonine Wall** itself – demonstrates that much of the surrounding countryside had been cleared of trees and was used for the pasturing of animals. There is little evidence for arable farming in Scotland at this time. Analysis of botanical remains suggests that the tree cover in the Roman period was not very different from today's, with a light covering of mixed deciduous woodland and a ground flora of herbaceous plants, mosses, shrubs and bracken growing at the edge of the woodland.

This scene on Trajan's Column shows an auxiliary soldier fighting. Soldiers like this guarded the northern frontier in Britain. The soldier wears mail over a shirt, with a kerchief at the neck. His head is protected by a helmet. His sword is worn on the right side and his right hand was holding a spear, now lost. His oval shield here is also being used as a weapon against his Dacian foe.

The fort on the Antonine Wall at **Rough Castle** from the air. The Antonine Wall ditch is clearly visible, crossing the photograph from top right to bottom left. To the right (south) is the square enclosure of the fort, surrounded by two ditches, with the annexe beyond. At the top right can be seen the low banks of a field system which appears, in part at least, to date to the Roman period. At least one other fort on the Antonine Wall is known to have had a similar field system beside it. Perhaps the farmers lived in the adjacent civil settlement.

The defensive pits in front of the north defences at **Rough Castle**. Pits like this were called lilies (*lilia*) by Caesar's soldiers. These pits are unique within the Roman Empire.

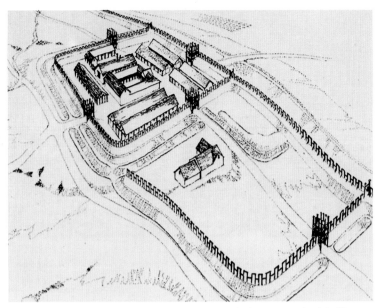

A reconstruction of the fort at **Rough Castle** by M J Moore. The fort is crammed with buildings, including the headquarters in the centre, with the granary and commanding officer's house beyond; the other buildings were barrack-blocks and stores. The bath-house lies in the annexe. There is little evidence concerning the use of annexes on the Antonine Wall. They may have sheltered animals or troops in transit; some housed industrial activities perhaps too dangerous to take place in the fort.

This inscription records the building of the fort at **Bearsden** by soldiers of Legion XX Valeria Victrix operating under the command of an officer whose name has been abbreviated to QUINT, perhaps Quintus or Quintianus. The legion was based at Chester, and sent a detachment to help build the Antonine Wall.

The bath-house at **Bar Hill** looking west, with the hot room (*caldarium*) in the foreground.

Quernstones, metal cooking pot, mess tin, pan and cooking pot from Newstead. Some of these items may have been supplied by the army; others were bought by the soldiers.

Wine jars from Newstead. These vessels were used to carry wine, oil, or other commodities such as prunes, beans and fish-sauce. Food was provided by the army, but money for it was deducted from each soldier's pay.

In the **Bearsden** area the predominant trees when the Romans arrived were hazel and alder, which were used in the construction of the fort's buildings.

The Romans appreciated the problems of disease in an army and thus every fort had its own bath-house and latrine for the use of all the soldiers in residence, while larger forts also contained a hospital. Medical staff included doctors, medical orderlies, bandagers and ointment-makers. Diet was carefully considered too. While wheat formed the staple part of the diet, the food included several different types of meat, fish and shell-fish, vegetables, fruit and nuts. New wine was the common drink.

Analysis of the sewage found beside the latrine at **Bearsden** demonstrates that the soldiers there ate wheat (both emmer and spelt), which was presumably made into bread or gruel. Fragments of barley resemble the pearl barley used nowadays in broth. Coriander, dill, celery, linseed and opium poppy were used not only in cooking but also medicinally. Fruit eaten included figs, raspberries, blackberries, bilberries and strawberries; hazelnuts also appeared on the menu. Many of these items could have been obtained locally, but others such as opium poppies and figs are not native to Britain and must have been imported from the continent. Analysis of the food debris indicates that the soldiers had a mainly vegetarian diet. They also suffered from worms!

Other items used by the Roman soldiers were brought from far afield, including armour and weapons (produced in the army's own factories), tools and clothing, pottery and cooking equipment. Surviving military documents indicated that soldiers might travel several hundred miles to procure supplies. Other products could have been

A reconstruction of the bath-house at **Bar Hill** by M J Moore. The changing room is at the far end and the heated rooms are in the block to the right.

The bath-house at **Bearsden**, looking south. The main spine of the building runs east-west. The bather entered the timber changing room (right); this led into the central, or cold, room. Here the bather was faced with a choice between continuing onward into the steam range, or turning left into the hot dry room. The heating was provided by hot air warmed by fires lit in furnaces. After taking either treatment the bather could take a dip in the cold bath (the apsidal room). The latrine lies top left.

Roman leather shoes found at Newstead.

obtained locally. These include wood for building, bracken and heather for bedding, marsh hay for fodder, and wood and peat for fuel. The Roman army also required large quantities of leather for making into tents, shoes, bags, shields, shield-covers and saddles: hides would certainly have been obtainable locally.

It is possible that the presence of the Roman army, with its major demands for food and goods, encouraged local agriculture, but there is little evidence for this in Scotland. There is evidence, however, for a growth in the size and number of native farms during the Roman period, and this may be related not only to the peace, or *pax*

Romana, imposed by the Roman army but also to the army's supply needs.

Regulations governed the payment for goods supplied to the army, but there is also plenty of evidence from other frontier areas of the empire for extortion and corruption by soldiers. There can be little doubt that the situation would have been similar in Britain.

The fort was the unit's base and home. Through many months of the year, however, soldiers would be out on patrol, escorting supplies, serving on guard duty in the provincial headquarters in London and later in York, and perhaps even

The Roman road, **Dere Street**, which led north along the line now taken by the A68. Beside the road are scoops – pits from which the gravel was dug to build the road. This view, looking south, shows the road crossing Soutra.

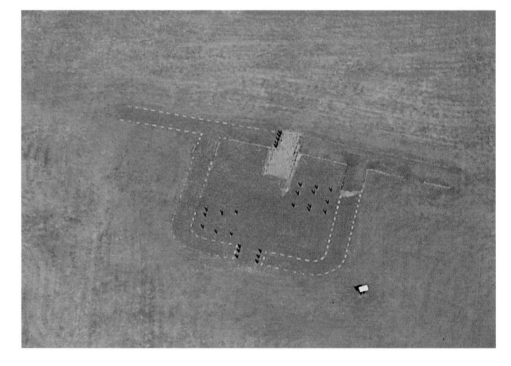

The fortlet at Kinneil from the air. The fortlet is attached to the rear of the Antonine Wall and a road passed through the fortlet and the Wall, here represented by a grassy bank. Within the fortlet a timber building (represented by posts) lay on each side of the road. These houses the soldiers charged with the duty of guarding the access point to the empire.

fighting. Some were outposted for several years to fortlets, while others manned watch-towers and signal-stations. Within the province the army served as the empire's police force, maintaining law and order in the frontier area. The regimental commanding officers served as local judges, acting rather as the British Empire's district officers were later to do. Training was another important part of military life, and in the 3rd century the abandoned hill-fort on Burnswark was apparently used for training soldiers in the use of catapults and similar engines of war.

When on campaign soldiers protected themselves

by constructing a camp. Within this, their tents (of leather) were arranged in rows according to strict regulations. Marching camps would usually be occupied for no more than about three days, for in that time the soldiers are likely to have contaminated the water supply and eaten all the food in the area. Soldiers involved in building projects, such as the construction of the **Antonine Wall** or permanent forts, also lived in camps.

The Roman army preferred to fight a set-piece battle, as it was specially trained for this type of warfare and was usually successful. Mons Graupius was such a battle, though tactically

The Antonine Wall passes round the front of an Iron Age hill-fort on **Castlehill** immediately to the east of **Bar Hill**. In this view the Antonine Wall ditch enters the photograph bottom right, crosses diagonally, curving round the hill-fort to leave top left. The rampart and ditch of the hill-fort survive now as a low terrace, and it is probable that it was already abandoned when the Romans arrived.

This settlement of stone houses at **Ardestie** has attached to it an underground passage or souterrain. This chamber may have been used for storage. There are other souterrains of the Romano-British period at **Carlungie** and **Tealing** near by, while a contemporary settlement of stone-built houses is visible at **Edinshall**, near Duns (see *Scotland BC*).

speaking it was a relatively simple affair. On most other occasions the Caledonians seem to have adopted guerrilla tactics, a sensible, though ultimately unsuccessful, method of fighting the highly disciplined Roman army. The tribes south of the Tay do not appear to have caused the Romans any trouble. In fact, Tacitus took more space writing about the appalling weather of the year 79 than he did about the conquest of Agricola's opponents. The Caledonians and their successors, the Picts, were always the main enemy of Rome.

Civilians in the Frontier Zone

Roman soldiers were well paid. To their forts were attracted merchants, inn-keepers and women – in fact all those who wished to transfer as much as possible of the soldiers' pay into their own pockets. Little is known in Scotland of civil settlements, which we know sprang up outside forts elsewhere in the empire. At Inveresk, beyond the east end of the Antonine Wall, excavations has demonstrated that the buildings outside the 2nd century fort there were of timber, but were later replaced in stone. The layout suggests that the buildings were set out along the main street which left the east gate of the fort. One of the buildings here contained a furnace and was clearly used for industrial purposes. Other buildings in civil settlements would have been inns and shops, temples and houses. Although a Roman soldier was not allowed to marry according to Roman law, he might acquire an unofficial wife, and perhaps marry her according to local custom. This union was retrospectively recognised by the State when he retired. The wife and children presumably would have lived in the civil settlement; and sons often appear to have joined their father's regiment. Sometimes these civil settlements gained self-governing rights. One such case is known in Scotland, that at Carriden at the east end of the Antonine Wall.

We know of no other examples of local government in Scotland during any of the Roman periods; certainly no towns or cities seem to have been founded. The whole of the frontier zone was probably military territory, administered by the army.

The inhabitants of the civil settlements were wholly dependent on the army and would follow it wherever it led. There is no evidence that any of the settlements established outside forts in Scotland survived the withdrawal of the army in either the 1st or the 2nd century.

Surprisingly there is little tangible sign of contact between the soldiers and civilians of the fort, with its attendant village, and the people of the countryside. Some Roman objects found their way on to native farms, but relatively few. More artefacts were acquired by the higher strata of society, especially those who lived in the brochs and duns of southern Scotland. Many Roman objects have also been found on Traprain Law in East Lothian, which has led to the suggestion that the tribe whose capital that was, the Votadini, had a special treaty relationship with Rome.

The tribesmen of this northern frontier area must have been taxed by the Romans, as no doubt they had been by their previous masters. Taxation was

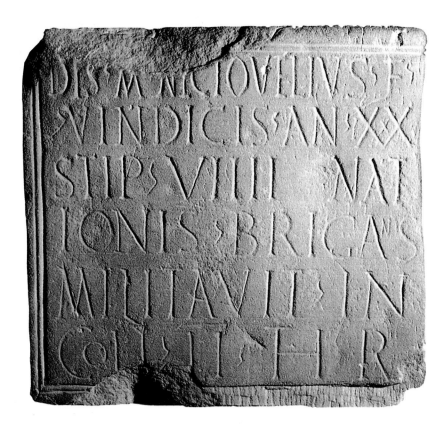

DIS·M·NECTOVELIVS·F
·VINDICIS·AN·XXX
STIP·VIIII·NAT
IONIS·BRICAS
MILITAVIT·IN
COH·II·THR

The tombstone of Nectovelius, a Brigantian, who served in Cohort II Thracum and died at Mumrills. This inscription neatly reflects the nature of the Roman army. The unit had been raised in Bulgaria. Once established in Britain, it recruited locally. Nectovellius had probably joined the regiment when it had served in the north of England, the territory of the Brigantes. Neither Romans nor other Italians served on the Antonine Wall.

usually in cash, though it might be in kind in frontier areas. Payment in hides and also recruits are attested on other frontiers. Some of the young men of the northern tribes may have joined the Roman army. (Most men joined the army between the ages of 18 and 21.) If they remained peaceful – and there is little evidence for warfare within the northern region of the Roman province – the local people may have had little contact with the army. The tribes beyond the frontier were different. As we have seen, they raided or invaded the Roman province on several occasions. One interesting aspect of the Roman records of these incursions is that the named tribes are reduced in number as the centuries pass. Thus by the 4th century we know of only one tribe beyond the Forth, the Picts, though this nation seems to have contained a number of divisions which may have reflected earlier tribes swept up into a new confederacy. Here may lie the major gift of Rome to the people of north Britain. The presence of a united political entity in the southern part of the island seems to have led to the amalgamation of the disparate tribes beyond the frontier, which then enabled them better to oppose the might of Rome. Certainly the Picts would need the strength formed from unity in the centuries ahead as they faced invasion by Scots from Ireland, Angles from Germany, and Vikings from Norway.

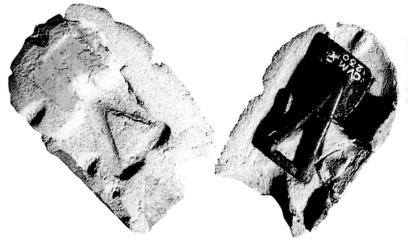

Moulds for the manufacture of dress-fasteners found at the native town on Traprain Law. These objects were sold to both civilians and soldiers in north Britain.

COLONISTS CROSS THE IRISH SEA – THE SCOTS CREATE A NEW KINGDOM IN ARGYLL

An Irish type of face-cross from Riasg Buidhe, now at Kiloran House, Colonsay.

DURING the Roman occupation of Britain, the lands north of the **Antonine Wall** belonged, as we have seen, to Celtic tribes whose unification finally led by the 6th century to the creation of a kingdom of the Picts. In the course of these political developments, much of Argyll, both mainland and the islands, was settled by Irish people from the nearest shores of County Antrim. According to historical tradition, this settlement took place around AD 500 and involved members of the Irish tribe known as the Dal Riata, led by Fergus Mor mac Erc (Fergus the Great son of Erc), who established in Argyll a new kingdom of Dalriada in answer to rival dynastic pressures in northern Ireland. The need for new territory is undoubted, but rather than a sudden migration of large numbers of people from Ireland to Argyll around the year 500 current opinion favours a gradual settlement from northern Ireland having taken place during the previous two centuries. There is certain archeological evidence for contact between Scotland and Ireland in this period in the form of imported artefacts, but perhaps the strongest argument lies in historical records of Scotti fighting alongside Picts against the Romans in north Britain in the 4th century. It seems more likely that these Irishmen were already living in north Britain than that they crossed the Irish Sea in large numbers at that time simply in the hope of rich pickings.

Whatever the background, an identifiable kingdom of Dalriada emerged in Argyll around 500, and the Scots' own perception of its foundations centres on a transfer of the ruling house. Historical sources indicate the extent of Dalriada by the 7th century: it stretched from the Mull of Kintyre northwards into Ardnamurchan and included the islands off the west coast and the lands around the eastern reaches of the long sea lochs. Important defended places are mentioned and can be identified as Dunollie (*Dun Ollaigh*) at Oban, **Dunadd** (*Dun Att*) south of Kilmartin, Tarbert (*Tairpert Boittir*) and Dunaverty (*Aberte*) at the south end of Kintyre. Excavations have confirmed that Dunollie and **Dunadd** were occupied in this period, although the early levels on Dunollie were much disturbed in later times when the medieval castle was built; similarly, the early fort at Tarbert is presumably masked by the extensive medieval fortifications. **Dunadd** and Dunollie figure in monastic annals as places that were attacked or besieged periodically, with the clear implication that they were centres of power among the Scots.

The Scots spoke Gaelic, a Celtic language related to but quite distinct from the Celtic languages spoken by the Picts and the Britons. The earliest Gaelic placenames in Scotland reflect not only the historically attested settlement of Irishmen in Argyll but also an intensive settlement of the Rhins of Galloway of which contemporary history has nothing to tell. These are names containing the Gaelic element sliabh, meaning hill (such as Sliabh Gaoil in Argyll), which in Galloway often takes the form slew, as in Slewcairn. Such names are very common in the Rhins of Galloway, and there is archeological evidence for contact between this area and Ireland, its near neighbour across the Irish Sea, from the 6th and 7th centuries onwards.

Dunadd

The rocky hill of **Dunadd** was an ideal location for a fort. It rises entirely isolated from the flat boggy land surrounding it, making surprise attack impossible and a siege uncomfortable. The River Add meandering past gave access to the sea on Loch Crinan. **Dunadd** was geographically central

SCOTS AND GAELS
The term Scots comes from Latin *Scotti*, which means simply Irishmen. Some modern historians prefer the term Gaels, reserving Scots for both Gaels and Picts from the 10th century onwards.

Opposite
Dunadd, Argyll, a major Dalriadan fort of the 7th to early 9th centuries.

Dunadd, from the summit. The River Add can be seen meandering past.

in the kingdom and, although not permanently resident, the king and his retinue are likely to have stayed here regularly. The normal pattern for royal life at this time was a progress between the various royal houses; most of the king's revenue would have been in the form of food and drink, and this was the best way to ensure their enjoyment, as well as maintaining a visible royal authority.

Dunadd has been excavated on several occasions since the beginning of the twentieth century, most recently in the 1980s, and a reasonably full picture of the lifestyle of its inhabitants has emerged. The lay-out of the fort shows that full advantage was taken of the shape of the hill, with an inner citadel built on the western summit and a series of walled enclosures following the natural terraces below. The main entrance above the foot of the hill made use of a natural gully through the bedrock; with a massive wall on either side and presumably a timber superstructure over the great gates, this would have been a formidable sight.

The fort as we see it today is, however, the end-product of more than one phase of building, and the precise sequence by which its final lay-out evolved is not yet clear. Essentially it began its history as a small fort or dun on the western summit, which later became the inner citadel of a much larger establishment. The original dun enclosed an oval area, some 20 m by 13 m, and the south-west end was later extended into the present pear-shape.

The important status of Dunadd among the Scots is underlined by a series of carvings on the bare bedrock immediately in front of the inner citadel. These include a rock-cut basin, two shallowly carved footprints, an incised boar and an ogham inscription. (Apart from the basin, the carved surface visible today is an ingenious casting of artificial stone which protects the original surface below.) Between the boar and one of the footprints there is a lightly carved figure of a man smoking a pipe, which is known to have been made earlier this century. The earlier carvings are likely to date from the 7th and 8th centuries. Both the boar and the ogham inscription are more likely to be Pictish than Scottish and probably relate to some episode, perhaps a marriage alliance, in the relations between the two people. Although the ogham alphabet was invented in Ireland, this inscription is not in Gaelic and has yet to be translated satisfactorily.

The basin and the footprints should probably be associated with the ceremonies surrounding the inauguration of kings and chieftains: ritual anointing and the symbolic stepping into the shoes of predecessors are familiar features of such inaugurations. Carved footprints have also been found at Southend in the Mull of Kintyre, close to the fort at Dunaverty, and at Clickhimin in Shetland; and a rock-cut hollow or basin exists high within the Scotto-Pictish fort of Dundurn in Perthshire.

It seems that there were special occasions in the life of Dunadd, but what of the everyday activities of its inhabitants? Soil conditions mean that bone does not survive well, but we can assume that animal products were used (meat, milk, skins and

bone), and plant remains show that wheat, barley, oats and hazel-nuts were among the crops enjoyed as food.

More than 50 quernstones from rotary hand-mills have been found, mute testimony to the long hours spent reducing grain to flour. This was perhaps one of Dunadd's few disadvantages: had there been suitable water-courses in the vicinity, those tedious hours of grinding could have been replaced by the service of water-mills. Iron was being worked in the fort for the manufacture of weapons and tools, some of which were used in carpentry and in leather-working. Fine bronze jewellery was also made here, for there are many fragments of the small crucibles in which the metal was melted and of the clay moulds in which pins and brooches were cast. Many of the brooches were made to designs fashionable throughout Pictland as well as Dalriada in the 8th century. There are also sketch designs on pieces of slate, which bring us closer to the craftsmen themselves.

The footprints at **Clickhimin**, Shetland.

Left
Dunadd. Beyond the footprint (of a shod foot) are carved a boar and an ogham inscription.

Among the most interesting finds are those that tell of the contacts between **Dunadd** and the outside world. Imports such as the garnet in its gold filigree setting that was probably made in an Anglo-Saxon workshop somewhere in England in the 6th or 7th century – what story lies behind its presence in this royal centre on the western fringes of Britain? There are scraps of imported glass for the jeweller to use as inlays on brooches. Above all there are broken sherds of mass-produced pottery from France, typical of a wide-ranging trade that was flourishing along the shores of the Irish Sea in the late 6th to 8th centuries.

Two very unusual discoveries serve to link **Dunadd** with the world of early Christianity. One is a small stone disc inscribed I(N) NOMINE 'in the name (of the Lord)', and the other a small lump of yellow orpiment (sulphide of arsenic), a pigment used by monks in the illustration of manuscripts. The disc certainly implies a Christian owner, and the yellow pigment may even be a clue to the presence of a monk from Iona.

Christianity
One very important group of placenames reflects the widening influence of Gaelic-speakers from the 6th into the 9th century, particularly in relation to the Christian Church. Names beginning with Kil, such as Kildonan and Kilmalcolm, contain the Gaelic element *cill*, meaning cell or church, often combined with the

name of the saint to whom the local church was dedicated: Kilmaluag on the island of Lismore near Oban was the church of St Moluag (or Moluoc), an Irish monk of the 6th century. Such names are very common in western Scotland from Skye southwards to Galloway and Dumfriesshire, and they extend eastwards across central Scotland to Fife and up the Great Glen into Easter Ross and Sutherland. They are the legacy of the Irish missionaries who converted the Picts in the 7th century and founded monasteries and churches in Pictland, and their eastern distribution reflects faithfully the links between Picts and Scots that can be seen in the artistic traditions of metalwork and sculpture. In particular, the close similarities between the high crosses of Iona, the great cross-slab at Nigg on the coast of Ross-shire and the sarcophagus at **St Andrews** on the Fife coast (see *Picts* p 40) form an ecclesiastical triangle of shared artistic skills and tastes.

The monastery on **Iona** was founded in or soon after AD 563 by St Columba, an Irishman of royal descent, born in County Donegal and trained for the priesthood, who crossed the Irish Sea with twelve companions. Iona's influence was to be far-reaching, both during Columba's own lifetime and throughout the 7th century, in the conversion of Pictland and of Anglian Northumbria. For Dalriada, the emergence of **Iona** as a major seat of Christian learning must have had an invaluable effect in stabilising and unifying the Scottish kingdom, although it could not prevent the inter-dynastic squabbling of the 7th and 8th centuries. It also ensured that relations with the Picts were not confined to the battles and sieges mentioned in historical sources.

During the years 688-92, not quite a hundred years after Columba's death, a later abbot of **Iona**, Adomnan, wrote an account of the saint's life. Most of this account is concerned with miracles and prophecies demonstrating Columba's saintliness, but there are also very useful glimpses of contemporary life. There are few visible remains of Columba's monastery on **Iona** but Adomnan mentions enough about its buildings to allow some impression of its lay-out. Apart from the church, there was a guest-house, a communal house for the monks, which probably contained the kitchen and dining-hall, and a series of small cells or huts in which the monks worked or slept. Columba himself had one cell for sleeping, 'having for his couch the bare rock, and for his pillow a stone', and another cell in which he wrote and from which he could see across the sound to Mull. After his death in 597, Columba's grave was marked by the stone that he had used as a pillow. (The grave no longer survives, because his bones were later dug up and revered as saintly relics.) All these buildings, together with several wooden high crosses, were enclosed within a substantial ditch with a bank on either side, part of which can still be seen today. Beyond were the fields and pastures that supplied the monks with food: cereal crops were grown, doubtless along with fruit and vegetables, and cattle, sheep and pigs were kept, the milk and meat supplementing the many fish that could be caught in the sea.

The island of **Eilean Mor** lies in the middle distance, with Jura beyond.

Excavations at **Iona** have uncovered traces of timber buildings, hearths and working areas which are thought to be at least as early as Adomnan's own time. Rare evidence of wood- and leather-working survived in a water-logged ditch; lathe-turned wooden bowls and stave-built buckets were used in the early 7th century, and fine leather shoes and small bags were made in the workshop from which offcuts of leather and the worn-out soles of old shoes also survived. High-quality metal-working was also practised, producing decorative mounts for leather book-bindings and wooden caskets. Stone-carvers made gravestones for the cemetery; a very large collection of Early Christian gravestones exists on **Iona**, from simple cross-marked slabs to free-standing crosses. The magnificent high crosses belong to the 8th century and later.

History and archaeology combine on **Iona** to sketch out a model of the lay-out and lifestyle of an early monastery, which is very helpful in understanding other monastic sites. Two smaller

monasteries are in State care, one on the island of **Eilean Mor** in the Sound of Jura and the other on one of the islands of the Garvellachs group to the north of Jura, **Eileach an Naoimh**. Both continued in use into medieval times, but there are traces of the earlier monasteries. On **Eilean Mor**, the early enclosure survives, along with three grave-markers which may be 7th or 8th century in date and a large free-standing cross which probably belongs to the 9th or 10th century. The head of the cross is unfortunately missing, but the shaft is decorated with human and animal figures. This monastery, itself isolated, had its own retreat: a cave some 250 m to the south, small and dark and ideal for solitary meditation. A cross of 7th-century type has been carved on its wall. Such caves were much in favour among early Christian ascetics and are often associated by tradition with particular saints; this one is associated with St Abban, one near Whithorn with St Ninian, one near Ellary in Argyll with St Columba, and several others are known.

Below left
Eileach an Naiomh, 'the island of the saint'.

Below right
Eileach an Naiomh. The monk's cell is a unique survival of the early monastery.

Eithne's Grave on Eileach an Naiomh

Above right
The high cross at **Kildalton**, Islay, superb testimony to the strength of early Christianity in Scotland.

Two very special features make the monastery on **Eileach an Naoimh** remarkable: an almost intact sleeping-cell and a circular burial-place. The cell is in fact a double building, with two interconnecting circular rooms, built of stone with corbelled domes of overlapping slabs. It lies at a short distance from what appears to have been the early monastic enclosure, but a small underground chamber within the enclosure may have been associated with a similar cell. The small chapel that stands roofless in this enclosure is not the original church but was built in the 11th or 12th century. A gully leads down from the monastic enclosure to the landing-place, past a natural spring known as St Columba's well; the remains of two lines of walling across the gully at intervals may belong to the early monastery. The monks were buried to the west of the main enclosure, in a cemetery in which a number of early grave-markers have been found, while further west lies the small circular enclosure traditionally – and wishfully – identified as the burial-place of St Columba's mother, Eithne. It has a distinct kerb of flat slabs, and one of three small upright slabs lining the inside of the kerb is incised with a cross. (The inner burial-space has not been excavated.)

The medieval and later remains on **Eileach an Naoimh** are also of interest and include the church, a dwelling-complex, a barn, a corn-drying kiln and various enclosures, taking the history of the site into the 19th century.

Elsewhere, the likely presence of an early Christian monastery can often be inferred from the survival of carved stones. A large number of early gravestones at Cladh a' Bhile (burial-ground of the sacred tree), at Ellary in Argyll, for instance, implies

that there was a monastery here in the 8th century. At a similar date there must have been a monastery at **Kildalton** on Islay and perhaps a little later at **Keills** in Knapdale, mainland Argyll, at each of which places there survives an outstanding high cross related to the 8th- and 9th-century crosses of **Iona**. There are no traces of contemporary structures, but such important sculptures would have been commissioned by a major ecclesiastical community, perhaps with lay funding.

Set among the trees in a quiet valley at the south end of the island of Bute, **St Blane's Chapel**, Kingarth, is a fine Romanesque church, built in the 12th century in a place by then long venerated as an early Christian monastery. St Blane himself is thought to have been born on Bute around 565, trained in the monastery at Kingarth (which must therefore have been founded almost as early as **Iona**) and sent as a missionary into southern Scotland and northern England. No trace survives of the church in which he worshipped, but the later church may well have been built on the same spot; within the oddly shaped churchyard, it is noticeable that the medieval burials all lie to the south of the church, leaving a considerable area to the north in which earlier burials may lie beneath the turf. The church-yard itself is enclosed within a larger, presumably monastic, settlement with its own boundary wall; both churchyard wall and boundary wall were largely rebuilt in the late 19th century. Remains of domestic buildings line the western side of the valley, including a puzzling circular house with a very thick wall. Without excavation, the site is difficult to interpret, but historical references to two bishops in the 7th century and three abbots in the 8th are unambiguous testimony to the important status of this early monastery.

Dalriadan Society

If forts such as **Dunadd** and monastic centres such as **Iona** and **St Blane's** were the public faces of Dalriada, there was also a range of lesser establishments: the farmsteads of land-owning Dalriadans and the hermitages of the unsung ascetics of the Columban Church. Beneath these in the hierarchical social sequence must have been the myriad homes of peasants, undefended and virtually invisible to the archaeologist unless discovered accidentally. Earthfast slabs protruding through the turf among the sand-dunes of Machrins on Colonsay led to the discovery of one such peasant home dating to around 800 and consisting of circular huts with central hearths. But between Machrins and **Dunadd** there are many middle-range farmsteads, on land enclosed by stone walls (duns) and in lochs built on artificial platforms (crannogs). The latter were essentially single-family establishments, like the crannog in Loch Glashan, a few kilometres east of **Dunadd**, on which traces of a rectangular timber house contained imported pottery comparable to that from **Dunadd** itself. Duns could be equally small, single-family eyries perched on rock-stacks like Dun Fhinn in Kintyre, or the fortifications of slightly larger communities, inhabiting several houses within a defensive wall as at Kildonan in Kintyre.

During the 7th and 8th centuries, there were dynastic struggles for the throne within Dalriada itself, and external campaigns against both the Picts and the Angles. In the long term, the most important relationship was that between Scots and Picts, both in war and in peace, because this prepared both peoples for the takeover of Pictland by the Scots that was finally achieved by the Scottish king, Kenneth mac Alpin, around 843.

The details of this prolonged political dialogue are for the historian rather than the archaeologist to explore, but it must have been painfully clear even by 800 that increasing pressure from Viking raids would make western Scotland a less-than-ideal base for an ambitious royal dynasty. As with the earlier settlement of Argyll, it is likely that a certain degree of Dalriadan infiltration of Pictland had already been achieved through inter-marriage, trade and the activities of the Church, and this favourable situation was improved in 839 when the ruling Pictish king was killed in battle by the Vikings. **Iona** was abandoned in 807 by its abbot and most of its monks, who retreated to the monastery of Kells in Ireland, leaving only a few monks to cope with subsequent Viking attacks. An important new church was founded sometime before 820 at **Dunkeld** in the heart of Pictland, and it was to this church that some of the relics of St Columba were brought in 849; the rest were taken to Kells. Nothing survives of this early church, but the massive cross-slab now housed in the cathedral may well have stood originally within the early ecclesiastical precincts. **Dunkeld** would thus seem to have been the ecclesiastical centre of the combined kingdom of Picts and Scots, but its secular centre seems to have been at Forteviot in the Earn valley, where Kenneth mac Alpin died in 858. To judge by the one fragment of its structure that survives, a carved stone arch, the palace complex must have been magnificent, the church at least built of stone and embellished with the skills of Pictish sculptors. Visible from the royal palace was a superb stone cross at Dupplin, set on a terrace high above the north bank of the river Earn; and there are likely to have been others at Forteviot itself where the base of such a cross was found. The Dupplin cross has been on display in the Museum of Scotland in Edinburgh since 1998. From 2002 it will be housed in Dunning, Perthshire (**St Serf's Church**).

Dun at Kildonan, Kintyre

Above left
A motif-piece from **St Blane's**, Kingarth: the work perhaps of a monk practising his skills. There is a panel of careful interlace on the left, alongside an initial letter.

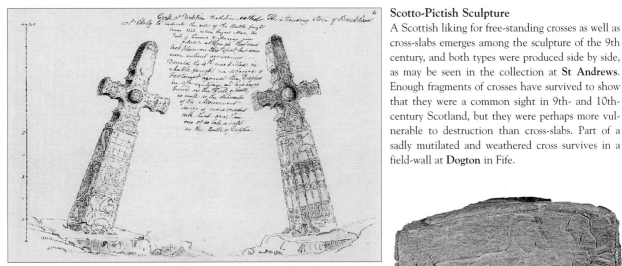

The great cross at **Dupplin**, Perthshire, drawn by J Skene in the early 19th century.

Right
Meigle stone no 26, side: a human knot.

Scotto-Pictish Sculpture

A Scottish liking for free-standing crosses as well as cross-slabs emerges among the sculpture of the 9th century, and both types were produced side by side, as may be seen in the collection at **St Andrews**. Enough fragments of crosses have survived to show that they were a common sight in 9th- and 10th-century Scotland, but they were perhaps more vulnerable to destruction than cross-slabs. Part of a sadly mutilated and weathered cross survives in a field-wall at **Dogton** in Fife.

Meigle stone no 26:
an enigmatic image of pursuit.

The shaft of a free-standing cross at **St Andrews**, Fife.

Meigle stone no 26. This magnificent graveslab was surely created for someone of great importance. Not only the top but all four sides are decorated with a variety of beasts, birds, serpents and human figures, carved in relief with incised details.

Dunblane Cathedral.
Upturned animal-heads embellish the base of the cross.

The great Pictish workshops continued in production, as ever open to new ideas – such as the splendidly moustachioed warriors on the Dupplin cross, the Forteviot arch and, less grandly, on a small graveslab at Benvie near Dundee. The major impact of the Scottish political takeover on sculpture was the banishment of the characteristic Pictish symbols, clearly no longer appropriate. The two symbols on the side of **Meigle** stone no 5 must be among the last to be carved, and **Meigle** itself perhaps one of the last strongholds of Pictish culture. Despite the size of the collection in the **Meigle** museum, there is not one fragment of a free-standing cross; yet highly decorated gravestones continued to be carved into the late 10th century.

A 9th-century cross-slab at Benvie, Dundee. Two armed warriors on horseback sport magnificent drooping moustaches.

The declining art of the Pictish sculptor is clearly seen in the confused decoration on the back of the **Dunblane** slab, which includes, on the left, a free-standing cross of Irish Type.

Benvie, Dundee. The cross is flanked at the top by angels and below by pairs of entwined animals.

A HUNGER FOR LAND AND POWER –
THE ANGLES MOVE INTO SOUTHERN SCOTLAND

> Three hundred men hastened forth,
> wearing gold torques, defending the land –
> and there was slaughter.
> Though they were slain they slew,
> and they shall be honoured till the end of the world.

THUS sang the poet Aneirin of a famous battle between the Britons of Gododdin with their allies and the Angles of Bernicia and Deira. The battle took place at Catraeth (Catterick) in Deiran territory around AD 600 or slightly earlier, and it was the first recorded attempt to prevent the Anglian occupation of southern Scotland. Three hundred British warlords set out on horseback from Din Eidyn (Edinburgh), each with his warband of foot soldiers, but their defeat was total. Recognising the common danger, the Scots of Dalriada led a great army against the Bernicians in 603 and were defeated in their turn. The Anglian advance was unstoppable south of the Forth, and in 638 Edinburgh itself was captured, marking the end of the kingdom of the Goddodin.

The British kingdom of Strathclyde remained largely intact, but the Angles took over Rheged, penetrated into Galloway, and even advanced into Pictland, crossing the Forth to occupy Fife. The two Anglian kingdoms of Deira and Bernicia had been fused into one in 605, and the new kingdom of Northumbria stretched, for a few decades in the mid-7th century, from the Humber to the Tay and perhaps beyond.

In 685, however, King Ecgfrith of Northumbria over-reached his resources. Having sent an army across the Irish Sea and 'brutally harassed' the Irish the previous year, in the words of Bede, Ecgfrith 'rashly led an army to ravage the province of the Picts'. He and most of his army were slaughtered by the Picts at the Battle of Nechtansmere, not far

Birds and animals perch in a grapevine on the Anglian shrine in **Jedburgh**.

from Forfar (see *Picts*, pp 25-7), and the Angles were forced to abandon their occupation of Pictish lands. Bede tells us also that 'the Scots living in Britain and a proportion of the Britons themselves regained their freedom' as a result of this great defeat; these were probably the Scots and Britons of Galloway, for it was not until the early 8th century that a Northumbrian bishopric was established at **Whithorn**, in the old Celtic monastery.

Anglian settlement was strongest along the fertile plains of the east coast, and this is where the earliest Anglian placenames are to be found, along with archaeological evidence of these English-speaking newcomers. Three of the earliest settlements whose names have survived are

Opposite
Beneath the imposing walls of **Edinburgh Castle** lie traces of occupation at the time of the British fort of Din Eidyn.

Couldingham (*Coludingaham*, village of the people at Colud), Whittinghame (*Hwitingaham*, settlement of Hwita's people) and Tyninghame (*Tiningaham*, village of those dwelling by the River Tyne), all incorporating the elements *-ingas*, people, and *-ham*, settlement. Both Coldingham and Tyninghame are known to have had important Anglian Monasteries.

Excavation has identified the probable location of the monastery of Coldingham, not on the site of the medieval church but on Kirk Hill on the coast near St Abb's Head. A place of great natural strength and with a good landing-place alongside, Kirk Hall seems to have been fortified by a timber palisade as a secular stronghold in the 7th century, before becoming a monastic establishment enclosed by a bank and ditch. Archaeological, historical and placename evidence combine neatly in the case of Coldingham. Historical records point also to a Northumbrian stronghold at Dunbar, and recent excavations have uncovered traces of rectangular timber buildings on what was probably a fortified promontory.

The Halls of Princes

Substantial timber halls, fit for princely feasting, appears to have been a typical component of high-status settlements, both British and Anglian. Some impression of one of these halls is given in the Gododdin poem: before setting off on their mission, the warriors feasted for a year in the hall of Mynyddog, the British king whose stronghold was Din Eidyn, the forth of Eidyn, at Edinburgh. 'The men went to Catraeth, they were famous; wine and mead from golden vessels was their drink for a year, according to the honourable custom'. Mynyddog was also known as Mwynfawr, 'the wealthy' or 'the luxurious', which is just as well in view of the cost of such a prolonged entertainment. 'Never was built a hall so durable', the poet tells, the door open and welcoming, and within was 'the well-fed fire, the pine-logs blazing from dusk to dusk', and beside it the warriors reclined on couches covered with 'white fleece', drinking mead and wine from priceless beakers of glass, gold and silver as well as from horns.

Mynyddog's hall at Din Eidyn probably stood on the site of **Edinburgh Castle**, where limited excavations have discovered traces of occupation in both Iron Age and early historic times. But the most complete evidence of such a hall was discovered at **Doon Hill**, near Dunbar, in the 1960s, where the outlines of the buildings can be seen today as concrete templates in the green turf of this wind-swept hill. Curiously, the princely settlement was built beside an earlier cemetery of cremated burials, to which the square enclosure may belong; perhaps this was a sacred spot in pre-Christian times. The first hall was built probably in the early 6th century by a British chieftain. It was fully 23 m long, with sturdy timber walls, bowed ends and a doorway in the centre of each long wall,

Artist's impression of the Anglian hall at **Doon Hill**.

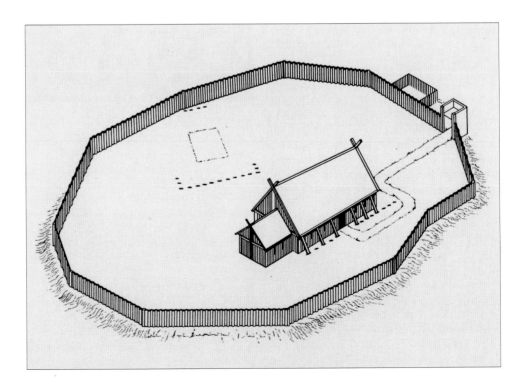

and it stood within a polygonal enclosure protected by a massive stockade of split logs and wooden fencing. This hall had been repaired several times and was finally destroyed by fire. The destruction may well have been at Anglian hands around AD 638 when history records that Din Eidyn was besieged and taken by Anglian forces. Certainly the smaller hall that was built in place of the destroyed British hall on **Doon Hill** corresponds very closely in design to halls built at Yeavering in Northumbria around 640. The new building was rectangular with straight gables, to judge by its construction trenches. Although none of the posts or beams of these timber buildings survived, some of the iron nails that helped to hold them together were found, and it is clear even from their ground-plans that these were sophisticated products of the carpenters' skills. A small cemetery lies outside the gateway into the settlement.

Doon Hill does not appear in any historical record and the settlement was discovered by aerial photography. Several other settlements that may well be Anglian have been located from the air in south-east Scotland: for example at Sprouston in the Tweed valley and at Whitekirk in East Lothian. These are all likely to have been the homes of important people, while the bulk of the population, predominantly of British stock, probably lived in much the same sort of round, stone or timber houses as their prehistoric forebears.

Dunbar: aerial view of excavations in Castle Park. Traces of Anglian buildings were discovered, enclosed by a bank and ditch.

Sir Walter Scott's favourite view encompasses the site of the original monastery of Old Melrose, almost encircled by the river Tweed, and the Eildon Hills beyond.

Jedburgh Abbey. The Doomsday Stone, on which Christ in Majesty appears to a multitude of dead and tormented souls (carving displayed in the Visitor Centre).

Jedburgh Abbey: part of the end-panel of a magnificent Anglian shrine (in the Visitor Centre).

This fragment from the gable of the shrine repeats the theme of the inhabited vine (in the Visitor Centre).

Anglian Sculpture at Jedburgh

Christianity was well established among the Britons of south-east Scotland, and a number of inscribed memorial stones survive from the 6th and 7th centuries in places such as Peebles and Ingliston (near Edinburgh) where there were Christian communities. In the case of Old Melrose, the Northumbrian monastery established in the later 7th century may have been a development of an earlier Christian centre of British origin; Bede describes the early years of St Cuthbert in the monastery at *Mailros*, a British name meaning 'bare promontory'. The 12th-century Cistercian abbey was founded further along the Tweed at **Melrose**, and there has been no excavation on the site of Cuthbert's monastery. In contrast, the collection of 8th- to 10th-century Anglian sculpture at **Jedburgh** points to the existence of a church or even a monastery there before the Augustinian abbey was founded in the 12th century. Most of the stones to be seen in the Visitor Centre and in the Stone Display Room at the west end of the abbey church were found built into the abbey or into nearby houses in the town. They include one, the Doomsday Stone, which was found during excavations in 1984, trimmed for re-use as a building slab. There is a marked contrast in style and technique between this slab and the rest of the carvings: deep incision creates an impression of low-relief sculpture, and the design is somewhat crude, yet powerful in its message. This style of carving was probably intended to provide no more than an outline, which was then further embellished by painting.

High-relief carving and a classic elegance of design mark the fragments of an 8th-century shrine, a stone box created to hold the relics of a saint; the tendrils of a vine curve into spirals in which birds and animals perch to feed on the grapes. This was a favourite Northumbrian motif and is known to art historians as the 'inhabited vine-scroll'. This must have been a magnificent shrine, but all that survives is the major part of one end-slab and a small fragment of the other; it appears to have been gabled. It has been argued that, since **Jedburgh** is not known to have been associated in the 7th or 8th centuries with anyone important enough to have been enshrined in such a box, the shrine originated at Old Melrose and was later brought to **Jedburgh** as building material. Too little is known about the early history of **Jedburgh**, however, to discount the greater probability that the shrine belonged to an early church at **Jedburgh** itself.

Fragments of cross-shafts and part of an ornate cross-head represent at least five free-standing crosses, all major pieces of sculpture of the 8th to 10th centuries. Such crosses may originally have slotted into simple stone sockets, but there is also at **Jedburgh**, in the garden of Queen Mary's House, an example of a more elaborate cross-base belonging to the early 9th century. All four faces of this substantial block of stone have been sculpted with pairs of animals and other motifs, and the top has been shaped into a tenon to fit the socket of a cross-shaft. It could have been the base for one of the crosses surviving as fragments in the **Abbey**. In

The 12th-century tomb in the south choir chapel at **Jedburgh** may have been put together using fragments of an earlier Anglian cross-shaft.

This reconstruction drawing shows the most likely original appearance of the **Jedburgh** Shrine.

the south choir chapel (also known as the Lady aisle), there is a tomb cover apparently constructed in the 12th century using two fragments of an earlier cross-shaft, decorated with interlace. These were tall slender crosses, surmounted by relatively small heads: the fragmentary cross-head illustrated here, consisting of the upper arm and central roundel, shows the type of ornate head that was carved in the early 9th century. The more massive proportions of a late 9th-century cross were appropriate for the large figures and thick cabling that decorated its shaft, four pieces of which survive; traces can be seen of the whitewash that was applied to the stone before its decoration was picked out in colour.

Enough Anglian sculpture has survived in southern Scotland, both from known sites of monasteries such as Coldingham and Abercorn and from places where a monastic presence must be assumed, to show the strength of the Church and of its artistic patronage. There had been a monastery at Abercorn since the 7th century, strategically placed in the southern shore of the Firth of Forth, the frontier between Pictland and Anglian territory; but the surviving sculpture, located in a storeroom at the east end of the church and including fragments of three fine crosses, dates to the 8th century and later.

The Ruthwell Cross

The most sophisticated memorial to the early church in Scotland is at **Ruthwell** (Nithsdale),

where there is no other evidence, archaeological or historical, for an early ecclesiastical presence. There was certainly an Anglian foundation at Hoddom, some 8 km away, and the great cross at **Ruthwell** may have been set up along the route between Hoddom and the Solway Firth.

The **Ruthwell Cross** was created in the early 8th century, undoubtedly by a master sculptor not only skilled in his craft but conversant with the

Left
One of several fragments of a cross-shaft decorated with human figures and animal interlace in panels, with a heavily-cabled border (in the Stone Display). This panel may depict the sacrifice of Isaac (right) by Abraham (left) **Jedburgh**.

Far left
The original cross, of which this is part of the head, must have been a work of great beauty (in the Stone Display) **Jedburgh**.

Ruthwell Cross
Both narrow sides of the cross-shaft are carved with vine-scroll in which birds and animals perch, and the margins are incised with Anglian runes.

major images of Christian art. The cross was demolished in 1642, but it was reconstructed in the 19th century and since 1887 has stood, fully 5.2 m high, within the parish church. Its front and back bear figural panels, each with its related Latin text alongside, illustrating episodes in the biblical account of the life of Christ. The sides of the shaft are filled with long panels of vine-scroll, inhabited as at **Jedburgh** by birds and animals, and the margins are carved with Anglian runes.

The runic alphabet was invented in Scandinavia, its vertical and oblique strokes designed for ease of cutting in wood, though it was also used on metal, bone, stone and ceramics. It was certainly in existence by the late 2nd century AD, but the precise date and place of its invention are uncertain. As the use of runes spread, local variations of the script developed and it was used for several different languages. In Britain we have Anglo-Saxon runes in England and southern Scotland (**Ruthwell, Whithorn**), and Norse runes in the areas settled by the Vikings, particularly northern and western Scotland and the Isle of Man (see pp 45-6).

The runic inscription of the **Ruthwell Cross** is written in Old English and records part of a very moving poem known also from a later manuscript, The Dream of the Rood. The rood is the cross on which Christ was crucified and the narrator is the cross itself:

> Almighty God stripped himself as he prepared to climb the gallows, valiant in men's sight...I raised up a great king, Lord of Heaven. I dared not bow down. Men reviled us both together. I was drenched in blood...Christ was on the cross. Yet to him in his solitude came noble men, eager, from afar. I beheld it all. I was bitterly troubled with griefs. I bowed... wounded with arrows. Down they laid that limb-weary one. They stood at the corpse's head. There they beheld...

The combinations of words and images. Latin and Old English languages, Roman and runic scripts make the **Ruthwell Cross** a most unusual and powerful monument – one that must have been remarkable even in its own day. The power and learning of the Church were here displayed, even for those who could not themselves read the inscriptions. The central panel on the front of the shaft depicts Christ in Majesty with his feet resting on two animals, and the Latin text on its margins reads: 'Jesus Christ the judge of equity. The animals and the serpents recognised the Saviour of the world in the desert.' The corresponding central panel on the back of the cross shows Mary Magdalene washing the feet of Christ: 'She brought an alabaster box of ointment; and standing behind [beside] his feet, she began to moisten his feet with tears, and with the hairs of her own head she wiped [them].

Ruthwell Cross
Right
Christ with His feet on a pair of animals, accompanied by the appropriate Latin text on the frame.

Centre Right
Mary Magdalene washing Christ's feet.

Far Right
St Paul and St Anthony break bread in the desert.

Other panels feature John the Baptist holding the Lamb, St Paul and St Anthony breaking bread in the desert, Mary and the Child on an ass fleeing into Egypt, the healing of the blind man, and the Annunciation.

Whithorn

At the time when the **Ruthwell Cross** was commissioned, in the early 8th century, Anglian political power was growing in south-west Scotland, to the extent that Bede, writing in AD 731, described **Whithorn** as belonging to the province of Bernicia. Whithorn was one of the earliest centres of Christianity in Scotland and was therefore a natural focus of interest for the Northumbrian Church. An episcopal seat had been established at Whithorn by St Ninian, sometime in the 5th century, though the precise date is unknown; and Bede tells us that it was 'commonly known as *Candida Casa*, the White House, because he built the church of stone, which was unusual among the Britons.' *Candida Casa* was Anglicised as *hwit erne*, hence the name Whithorn. By the 8th century, the famous home of St Ninian had become a magnet for pilgrims, and the Northumbrian Church was not slow to ensure that this important and influential monastery was controlled by an Anglian bishop. Not only Ninian himself but other saints as well were buried at Whithorn; one day, perhaps, archaeological excavation will discover fragments of some of these saintly shrines. The Whithorn Trust has been excavating to the south of the medieval priory since the mid-1980s, gradually building up a picture of daily life and of the changing burial customs from the time of Ninian until the 16th century. Particularly interesting is the evidence for Whithorn's participation in the trade network around the Irish Sea in the 6th to 8th centuries; fragments of mass-produced pottery and glass beakers imported from France illustrate the continental connections of a patron who could cause a fine cross-slab (no 2) to be inscribed in one of the contemporary scripts of Merovingian France.

Despite its absorption into the Northumbrian Church, Whithorn displays little Anglian influence on its surviving sculpture, perhaps because its own traditions of stone-carving were strong enough to resist the importation of Northumbrian craftsmen. There was certainly a Whithorn school of sculpture in the 10th and 11th centuries, characterised by disc-headed free-standing crosses which developed out of the encircled crosses carved on earlier slabs. The Monreith Cross (no 40 in the **Whithorn**

collection) is a fine example of a wayside prayer-cross of the Whithorn school in the 10th century.

The Scots Take Over Lothian

Officially, the Firth of Forth remained the boundary between the Scots and the Angles until AD 973, when Lothian was granted to the Scottish King, Kenneth II; but in practice the ousting of Anglian power was already well under way. One historical source states that the fort at Edinburgh was 'evacuated and abandoned to the Scots' sometime between AD 954 and 962, and reports of Scottish raiding south of the Tweed imply a freedom of movement in nominally Anglian territory. Northumbria had its own problems with the establishment of Scandinavian supremacy at York in the late 9th century, a situation of which the Scots undoubtedly took advantage. The Scottish hold of Lothian was later confirmed by Malcolm II's victory at the Battle of Carham around AD 1018.

Whithorn Priory, the medieval successor to St Ninian's church.

Norse traders settled at Whithorn in the 11th century; one of their houses has been re-created on the basis of the surviving traces found during excavation.

Whithorn. Inscribed in Latin, 'the place of Peter the Apostle', this cross-slab may originally have stood at the south gate of the 7th century monastery.

A MENACE IN THE NORTH – VIKING RAIDERS AND COLONISTS IN THE NORTHERN AND WESTERN ISLES

A Viking axe set on a modern wooden handle.

A DESPAIRING entry made by an Irish monk in his annal for AD 794 records the 'devastation of all the islands of Britain by the gentiles'. The 'gentiles' were the Norwegian Vikings who appeared off the Hebridean and Irish coasts in their longships and made swift, terrible and, for them, lucrative raids on monasteries and farms. These highly mobile Viking warbands probably operated from short-term bases in the Western and Northern Isles, and it has been suggested that the raid on the English monastery of Lindisfarne in 793 had been the work of Vikings based on Orkney rather than across the North Sea. 'Never before has such a terror appeared in Britain as we have now suffered from a pagan race, nor was it thought possible that such an inroad from the sea could be made', wrote an English churchman of Lindisfarne's catastrophe. In 795 Iona and Skye were devastated, along with monasteries in Ireland, and in 798 there were raids throughout the Hebrides and Ulster. Vikings returned to pillage Iona in 802, in 806 when 68 members of the community were killed, and in 825 when the monk Blathmac was put to death for refusing to reveal the hiding-place of the shrine containing St Columba's relics.

These are some of the recorded Viking raids and there must have been many more that were unknown to the annalists or that involved non-ecclesiastical targets considered unworthy of record. This was the first stage of Viking activity in Scotland, and it seems to have been followed swiftly by permanent settlement, not just by warriors but by wives and families as well. Settlement was most intensive in Orkney and Caithness, where a vigorous and powerful Norse earldom was to develop, and in the Outer Hebrides; but the effects both of raiding and settlement were felt throughout most of Scotland.

The Viking threat weakened Pictland and stimulated the Scots of Dalriada towards their eventual takeover of Pictland. Nor did Viking aggression stop with settlement. Viking Dublin was a major trading port and power-centre, and Viking warbands crossed the Irish Sea with confidence to harass their neighbours. There was raiding and hostage-taking in central Scotland in 866, when Olaf of Dublin is thought to have taken up residence there for several months, and in 870-1 Vikings attacked the British royal seat of **Dumbarton Rock. Dunkeld** and central Scotland were ravaged again in 903 and 904. Any hopes that the Norsemen may have had of establishing a power-base in the southern Scottish kingdom were consistently thwarted.

In northern Scotland the situation was different. The Norse earldom that was firmly established in the Northern Isles and Caithness by the later 9th century extended as far south as the River Oykell and the Dornoch Firth and possibly beyond. The first earl was Sigurd, brother of the powerful Earl Rognvald of Møre in Western Norway, and the history of the earls of Orkney is recorded in *Orkneyinga Saga*, a lively epic written by an Icelander around AD 1200. The saga is invaluable in providing an impression of the people and their lifestyle, particularly in Orkney where farms named in the saga can be identified with known archaeological sites. One account of the seasonal activities of a certain Viking illustrates very neatly the balance between farming duties and raiding adventures enjoyed even in the 12th century. Svein Asleifarson was a wealthy farmer on the Orkney island of Gairsay, and the saga-writer tells us,

> This is how Svein used to live. Winter he would spend at home on Gairsay, where he entertained some eighty men at his own expense. His drinking hall was so big, there

Opposite
Jarlshof, Shetland. Before excavations, only the ruined laird's house was visible, and it was to this that Sir Walter Scott gave the name Jarlshof in his novel, *The Pirate*.

was nothing in Orkney to compare with it. In the spring he had more than enough to occupy him, with a great deal of seed to sow which he saw to carefully himself. Then when that job was done, he would go off plundering in the Hebrides and in Ireland on what he called his 'spring-trip', then back home just after midsummer, where he stayed till the cornfields had been reaped and the grain was safely in. After that he would go off raiding again, and never came back till the first month of winter was ended. This he used to call his 'autumn-trip'.

Jarlshof house 1. The original building, consisting of kitchen and living-hall, was elongated by attaching a byre to one end. The narrow passage directed the cattle into their winter quarters, where stalls lay on either side of a central paved and kerbed strip. Beyond the byre extension, the raised benches of the original living-hall can be seen as low grassy platforms lining the walls.

Below
Jarlshof. Looking across to the Norse settlement from the top of the laird's house, it is easy to identify the principal house (1) by the white gravel with which it has been floored in modern times. The bay beyond gave shelter for boats and inshore fishing, while the light sandy soil alongside it allowed the growing of cereal and other crops.

Viking Age Settlements

Scotland is fortunate to possess well-preserved and visible Viking Age settlements at **Jarlshof** in Shetland and the **Brough of Birsay** in Orkney. Both were built on the sites of earlier native settlements (described in *Picts*), and this preference for old settlement sites seems to have been typical of most known 9th-century Norse establishments. Excavations on the **Brough of Birsay** have demonstrated a deliberate conformity on the part of the Norsemen to a pre-existing settlement pattern, with the result that the same building plots were used in pre-Norse, early Norse and late Norse times. There were presumably political reasons for this conformity, initially perhaps an attempt to underline the authority of the new Norse overlords in the eyes of the native population. In some cases, both here and at **Jarlshof**, existing buildings were taken over and modified, although for the most part the pre-Norse settlements appear to have been abandoned several decades previously.

The Viking Age farmstead at **Jarlshof** lies on the northern flank of the mound on which the laird's house now stands, an area that seems to have been on the periphery of the earlier settlement. The main dwelling-house (House 1) was built to an entirely new and distinctive Norse design. It was a rectangular building, fully 21 m long, with one of its side-walls slightly bowed; it was divided into

two rooms on either side of the main entrance, a large livingroom and a smaller kitchen, but the partition between them was probably no more than a wooden screen. This was the typical early Norse hall-house. In time this basic design was modified by the addition of a byre at one end (characterised at Jarlshof by paved flooring and narrow entrance-passages) and by small extra rooms built along the side-walls. The structural sequence is complicated and not entirely clear, but the mass of superimposed walls at **Jarlshof** illustrates the building, modification and re-building of an ordinary Norse farm over a period of some four or five hundred years, from the 9th to the 13th centuries. Beginning as the home of a single family, over the years the farm grew with the family and more dwelling-houses were needed until by the 12th century this was a very substantial farmstead. After it was finally abandoned, a new farmstead was built a little to the north-east in the 14th century; this consists of two rectangular buildings side by side, one the dwelling-house and the other a barn with a corn-drying kiln in one

Artist's impression of the interior of an early Norse dwelling-house.

Aerial view of **Jarlshof**, with the superimposed walls of the Norse settlement to the landward side of the Laird's house.

An iron spearhead and a stone whetstone from **Jarlshof**.

These bowls from **Jarlshof** are carved of steatite, or soapstone, an important natural resource in Shetland.

These bone dress-pins from **Jarlshof** are carved with fierce animal-heads in typical Viking taste.

Jarlshof. A carved handle, a dress-pin and a needle-case, all of bone.

Jarlshof. The gilded bronze mount (top) was probably a horse-harness ornament, while the trap-end (below) is decorated on both sides and is also gilded.

corner. This is a rare and very interesting example of a medieval farm, which seems to have continued in use until the first laird's house was built near by in the 16th century.

Excavations at **Jarlshof** have resulted in a large and varied collection of artefacts, some of which are in the site museum but most of which are in the Museum of Scotland in Edinburgh. They range from everyday equipment needed for cooking and processing food, for spinning, weaving and sewing cloth, for fishing and for mending boats, to more personal items such as knives, bone combs and jewellery. There are few weapons, but they would be treasured heirlooms either taken to the grave or melted down and re-made.

The medieval name for the area in which **Jarlshof** lies was *Svinaborg*, from which Sumburgh is derived, and this may be the name used for the Norse farm. It means either 'Svein's fort' or 'fort of pigs', and in both cases the fort could refer to the old broch, probably still an impressive ruin when the first settlers arrived. Whatever its name, neither the farm nor its family is mentioned in *Orkneyinga Saga*, whose author was more concerned with events in Orkney.

In contrast to **Jarlshof's** historical obscurity, the **Brough of Birsay** holds a major place in the early history of the earldom. It was already a power-centre in Pictish times and is likely to have been the seat of the local ruler, and, probably for that reason, was settled by Norsemen sometime in the 9th century. A tidal island, the **Brough** had obviously defensive advantages and yet was not isolated from its farming hinterland. The houses of the Norse settlers lay, like their native predecessors, on the landward slope of the island, overlooking the Bay of Birsay and the fertile lands that framed it.

Most excavated Norse settlements in Scotland have proved to be simple farms, even in cases where *Orkneyinga Saga* identifies the owners as people of wealth and social standing, but the settlement in the **Brough of Birsay** stands out as different from the rest. It was of high status and because of its island location it could not be, and clearly did not need to be, self-sufficient in terms of food-supply. The bulk of its meat and grain had to be imported from mainland farms. Excavations in the village of Birsay across the bay have revealed a large Norse barn with a corn-drying kiln at one end, which may have been involved in supplying grain or flour to the **Brough**. The community

living on the **Brough** was larger than the usual extended family unit – how large it is unfortunately impossible to gauge. There have been intermittent campaigns of excavation on the site over the last fifty years or so, and it is difficult to relate the results of the more recent and more scientific excavations to the old. Certainly the extent of the Norse settlement is considerably larger than the visible remains suggest: traces of houses and other buildings have been excavated along the eroding fringes of the island both to the north-east and to the south-west of the main site.

A likely sequence of events might be that the initial Norse settlement in the early 9th century was relatively small and that it expanded rapidly once it had become the political centre of the earldom in the early 11th century. *Orkneyinga Saga* records that Earl Thorfinn Sigurdsson 'had his permanent residence at Byrgisherad' (Birsay), and it seems likely that this was one of his family's properties even before Thorfinn made it his official residence.

The visible Norse buildings include simple hall-houses and later multi-roomed houses, as well as some unusual specialised buildings. One of these, set well away from the main focus of settlement, is a late Norse smithy, an essential industrial element in the community for the production and repair of iron tools and weapons. In the main settlement area, there are two unusually well-built small structures, known as Rooms VI and VII, which have both been interpreted as bath-houses or saunas, a component of wealthy households known from the sagas. These appear to be quite early in the building sequence. In keeping with the special status of the site, there are no longhouses, such as those at **Jarlshof**, with dwelling and cattle byre combined under one roof.

The visible settlement is dominated by the ruins of a fine church. This one building still arouses passionate argument: for some, this is the church that *Orkneyinga Saga* tells us was built by Earl Thorfinn at Birsay in the mid-11th century, but for others this is an early 12th century building and Thorfinn's church was situated on mainland Orkney in the village of Birsay. Whatever the truth, this was a well-designed and beautifully built Romanesque church of which the Brough community could be proud. Contemporary domestic buildings round a courtyard on the north side of the church are thought to have belonged to a small monastery, and the cemetery to the south contains slab-lined graves probably both of monks and of members of the secular community.

Brough of Birsay: There were defensive advantages in living on a tidal island.

The paved and walled entrance-way may also have been used as a boat-slip, on which boats could be hauled on wooden rollers out of reach of the sea.

Brough of Birsay. The bone comb is decorated with bronze rivets, and the long bone dress-pin has a hole to allow a cord fastening. The seal's tooth has been made into a pendant and is carved with the first six letters of the runic alphabet, probably as a magic formula.

A group of hall-houses aligned end-on to the southern slope of the island.

This carefully organised building may have been a sauna.

The church has a rounded apse at the east end.

The church consists of nave, chancel and apse, and there are traces of a porch or tower at the west end. A stone bench lines either long side of the nave.

Norse Strongholds

The builders of most of these Norse settlements paid little attention to defence other than by using the natural advantages of an island situation. In the Northern Isles at least, the Norse overlords could be confident of their political position, although there are hints of rivalry and even raiding amongst the leading Norse families. The great silver treasure that was buried amongst the sand-dunes of Skaill Bay in Orkney around 950 was recovered neither by its owner nor by the raiding party that had presumably prompted its concealment: it lay safely hidden until a boy caught a glimpse of objects thrown up in a rabbit scrape in 1858. (The treasure is now in the Museum of Scotland in Edinburgh.) On the whole it was simpler to take evasive action by escaping than to build fortified strongholds – although Orkneyinga Saga has many stories of people caught unawares and burnt along with their farms. Forts were built, however, on occasion. Orkneyinga Saga mentions a stronghold built in Moray by Earl Sigurd of Orkney in the late 9th century, and the ruins of two stone castles built by Norsemen in the 12th century survive today. One is the **Castle of Old Wick** in Caithness, a small tower perched on a rocky promontory along with its ancillary domestic buildings; the other is **Cubbie Roo's Castle** on the Orcadian island of Wyre. (The place of these castles in the wide context of early castle-building is discussed in another volume in this series, Scottish Castles and Fortifications.) **Cubbie Roo's Castle** lacks natural defence, and the stone tower and its domestic outhouses were therefore tightly encircled by a rock-cut ditch with a sturdy wall on the inner side and earthen rampart on the outer. Cubbie Roo is a nickname for Kolbein Hruga, and he and his castle have an admiring mention in Orkneyinga Saga, the implication being that such a castle was rare and prestigious among the Norsemen: 'At that time there was a very able man named Kolbein Hruga farming on Wyre in Orkney. He had a fine stone fort built there, a really solid stronghold.' This was around the year

The first recorded stone castle in Scotland, **Cubbie Roo's Castle** on Wyre, Orkney.

Cubbie Roo's Castle. Only the ground floor of the tower survives, and the sole entrance was on the first floor. The ground floor, accessible internally by ladder, was probably used for storage and a rock-cut water-tank is visible in the floor.

The Norsemen were very fond of board games – this stone board came from a 9th-century farm on the Point of Buckquoy, Orkney.

Right
Artist's impression of the grave of a Viking woman at **Gurness**, Orkney.

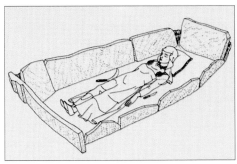

Moseyjarborg, the broch of **Mousa**, Shetland.

1150, making Kolbein's castle the earliest recorded stone castle in Scotland.

In the Isle of Man, Norsemen utilised existing native promontory forts, and this may also have happened in northern and western Scotland. Some brochs, the stone towers of the Iron Age, were sufficiently well preserved to serve as temporary refuges into medieval times. Clan tradition tells of the fate of cattle-raiders who sought protection inside the broch at **Carloway** on Lewis, only to be smothered by burning heather thrown down on them from the wall-top. The broch on **Mousa** in Shetland was certainly used in Norse times, for it is twice mentioned in Icelandic sagas as *Moseyjarborg*. In the spring of 1153, the broch was the scene of a famous siege, the story of which is told in *Orkneyinga Saga*. Earl Harald of Orkney's mother, Margaret, was 'a very beautiful woman but full of her own importance', and her hand in marriage was sought by Erlend the Young. Harald refused consent, whereupon 'Erlend raised a force of men, abducted Margaret from Orkney, took her north to Shetland and settled down in the broch at Mousa where everything had been made ready.' Earl Harald set off in pursuit and laid siege to the broch, cutting off all supplies, but he

soon found that it was 'not an easy place to attack' and was eventually persuaded to agree to a reconciliation: Erlend and Margaret were married, and Harald gained Erlend's support in his efforts to gain sole control of the earldom.

Viking Age Graves

There is archaeological evidence for the presence of Norsemen on the site of the old broch at **Gurness** in Orkney. During the 7th and 8th centuries there was a flourishing Pictish settlement here, but it is not known whether the site had been abandoned or was still occupied in the late 8th century when Viking longships first appeared in Eynhallow Sound. Along the coast a short way to the north of **Gurness**, a treasure of Pictish silver and amber was hidden in the ruins of another broch at Burgar, a sign perhaps of alarm and panic amongst the native population. (Discovered in 1840, this treasure was unfortunately later lost.) A number of Viking artefacts were found during excavations at **Gurness**, including iron shield-bosses, a merchant's folding balance and a glass linen-smoother, but it is not certain whether these represent a domestic settlement or gravegoods from disturbed Viking burials. One undoubted grave of a Norse pagan was excavated: the body of a woman had been buried in a stone-lined pit dug into the old rampart of broch times. She lay on her back, fully dressed, with her favourite jewellery and personal belongings; two oval brooches of bronze lay on her chest, the back of one brooch retaining traces of the fine woollen dress in which she had been buried. Around her neck was an iron necklet with a Thor's hammer pendant, and beside her were the iron sickle and iron knife that had been indispensable tools in life.

The remains of two long rectangular houses were also uncovered but neither is closely datable, and the domestic status of **Gurness** in Norse times must remain uncertain. The site would have been attractive with plenty of building stone, defences that could be renovated if necessary, good farmland and sheltered fishing. Across the sound, on Rousay, a known Viking Age farm has been excavated at Westness, with its cemetery close by.

Pagan Viking Age graves in Scotland belong to the 9th and 10th centuries and are concentrated in Orkney, Caithness and the Western Isles. These are the graves of the raiders, merchants and settlers of the first hundred years or so of Viking activity, and the personal belongings buried with them show a mixture of weapons, tools and jewellery brought from Norway and new finery, usually brooches and decorative mounts, acquired in the West as loot or barter. Some graves were stone-lined like that at Gurness, some were shallow pits and a few were splendid affairs, with the body placed in a boat and a great mound raised above it. Occasionally the skeleton of a horse is found, slaughtered to accompany its owner, and one woman was buried on Colonsay with her pet dog laid with its head on her knees.

As the Norse settlers gradually accepted Christianity in the course of the 10th century, pagan burial rites and the practice of leaving gravegoods with the deceased were dropped, to the disadvantage of the archaeologists for whom gravegoods are a useful means of dating. The Orkney earldom was finally and officially converted by order of the Norwegian king, himself a recent convert, in AD 995, probably as a political move to underline his authority. No pagan graves have yet been found on the **Brough of Birsay**, despite its settlement by Norsemen in the 9th century, but the graveyard contains many Christian graves which are probably contemporary with the 12th-century church. Similarly, the pagan cemetery belonging to **Jarlshof** has yet to be found; if it lay on the old broch-mound, it would have been destroyed by the construction of the first laird's house in the 16th century. Fragments of a 10th- or 11th-century memorial stone certainly suggests that the mound was used for Christian burials.

Norse Runes

The Vikings brought with them a new language, Norse, and a distinctive script, runes. The new language had an immediate and lasting effect upon placenames in northern and western Scotland, the earliest reflecting accurately the archaeological evidence for the areas first settled by Viking families as well as indicating the Norwegian homelands from which they came. Important early elements are *stathr* and *bolstathr*, meaning 'dwelling-place' or 'farm', as in Scarasta (Harris) and Scrabster (Caithness), and *setr*, meaning 'dwelling', as in Setter (Shetland). Such names are

The bronze brooches and iron sickle that were found in the **Gurness** grave.

Ring of Brodgar. Norse runes have been lightly carved on one of the broken standing stones of this prehistoric circle (the third stone to the north of the entrance).

Ring of Brodgar. The five runes are a cryptogram for a man's name, Biorn (modern Bjorn), and beneath is a simple Christian cross.

The chamber of the neolithic tomb of **Maes Howe**, Orkney, has many runic inscriptions on its walls.

Right
The **Maes Howe** runic graffiti are informal, often light-hearted messages.

Runic inscription in **Maes Howe**, using both ordinary runes and tree runes.

plentiful in the Northern Isles, Caithness and the Western Isles, and they combine with the archaeological evidence of graves and settlements to show that these were the primary areas settled in the 9th century. Comparable placenames in Norway occur along the west coast, particularly the area between Bergen and Trondheim but also extending southwards. The Viking settlers in Scotland named their new homes and surroundings with the words familiar to them, and their language rapidly replaced that of the native inhabitants. Norse remained the language (known as Norn) of the Northern Isles until the 16th century and later, when it was superseded by Scots, but Norse was overtaken by Gaelic in medieval times in the Western Isles. Nevertheless, 99 out of 126 village names on Lewis have remained purely Norse.

The Norsemen used their own runic script (see p 34) for graffiti such as those in **Maes Howe**, for memorial stones such as that found on **Iona**, and for brief inscriptions on small personal belongings, such as the seal's tooth amulet discovered during excavations on the **Brough of Birsay** (see p 41). The latter is probably 9th or 10th century in date to judge from its context, but an isolated graffito such as that at the **Ring of Brodgar**, also in Orkney, is difficult to date. The thirty or so inscriptions on the walls of **Maes Howe** comprise the largest known collection of runes carved on stone; they are exceeded in number only by the runes carved on wood found during urban excavations in Bergen, Norway.

Maes Howe is a stone-built tomb inside a huge earthen mound, and it was built around 2700 BC. In the 12th century AD, Norsemen broke into the burial chamber through the roof, and it seems likely that it was entered on several occasions thereafter. Not only do the runes betray the Norsemen's presence but there is also an historical record in *Orkneyinga Saga* which tells of one of these visits. It happened at a time when two rival earls were trying to out-manoeuvre one another for control of the northern earldom. Early in January 1153, Earl Harald and a party of men were crossing mainland Orkney on foot from Stromness to Firth, hoping to surprise Earl Erlend: 'During a snowstorm they took shelter in Maes Howe and there two of them went insane, which slowed them down badly, so that by the time they reached Firth it was night-time.' The Norse name for **Maes Howe** was *Orkahaugr*. That occasion was perhaps too traumatic to have given rise to any graffiti-carving, but a more suitable time may have been found the following winter when men were

Inchcolm. The hogback tombstone in its original location (it has been moved inside to protect it from the elements).

gathering to prepare for a trip to the Holy Land: 'Jerusalem-farers open this mound,' states one of the runic inscriptions.

Many of the inscriptions are very carefully and skilfully executed, using both ordinary runes and cryptographic twig runes. Indeed one inscription boasts, 'These runes were carved by the man most skilled in runes in the western ocean'! This is carved on the left-hand side of the cell which opens on the south side of the main chamber, and it continues on the lintel over the cell entrance, 'with the axe which belonged to Gaukr Trandilsson in the south of Iceland'. The slaying of Gaukr Trandilsson in the 10th century is described in Njals Saga, and it has been argued that his axe stayed in the family of his murderer and was used, some 200 years later, to carve runes in **Maes Howe.**

Several inscriptions mention treasure: 'It is long ago that a great treasure was hidden here.' Yet the original prehistoric burials were too early to have been accompanied by any gold or silver gravegoods that Norsemen could have considered as treasury. However, there is archaeological evidence for repairs to the outer bank surrounding the mound in the 9th century AD, and it is possible that the tomb was re-used at that time for the burial of some wealthy Viking, along with his treasure.

Hogback Tombstones

There is another very distinctive Scandinavian legacy in Scotland: a type of recumbent tombstone known from its shape as the 'hogback'. The classic hogback is a massive block shaped like a house, with side-walls, gable ends, and a shingled (i.e. wooden-tiled) roof with a humped ridge; this curving ridge gave rise to the term 'hogback'. It was designed to be a monumental gravecover, and the fashion developed in the 10th century in the areas of Northumbria that had been settled by the Norsemen. It spread quickly into southern and eastern Scotland and, by the 11th century, there were examples in the Northern Isles, underlining the links between the northern earldom and south-east Scotland. Some, like those at Govan (Glasgow), Brechin (Angus, see p 53) and **Inchcolm**, have elaborate decoration including animals, but most are simply carved with roof-tiles, such as the splendidly humped example at Abercorn. Apart from the giants at Govan, these hogbacks are mostly too short to cover the entire length of an adult grave, but they may have been accompanied by a headstone.

The hogback on **Inchcolm** in the Firth of Forth is not only the earliest survivor of such tombstones in Scotland but also the sole example that is known to have been almost certainly in its original 10th-century position. It lay on a knoll above the medieval abbey and, in the 16th century, a stone cross stood beside it.

W. Stewart recorded in his *Buik of the Croniclis* of Scotland,

As I myself quhilk hes bene thair and sene.
Ane croce of stone thair standis on ane grene,
Middis the feild quhair that tha la ikone,
Besyde the croce thair lyis ane greit stone;
Wnder the stone, in middis of the plane,
Thair chiftane lyis quhilk in the feild wes slane.

The hogback is unfortunately now very weathered but must once have been very impressive, with a beast at either end, a truly humped back, carved rows of roof-tiles and, central to each long side, a human figure and a cross respectively.

True to the independent spirit of earlier sculptors in Scotland, the creator of the **Meigle** hogback (no 25) adapted the basic design to suit the sandstone block at his disposal, with the result that the tombstone is wedge-shaped. At the high end, an animal head gazes out from the ridge, its ears lying flat, and the decorated ridge runs down to finish in a fishtail above the tip of the wedge. The animal-head is very similar to those at the base of the cross on **Meigle** cross-slab no 5.

Within the Norse earldom of Orkney and Shetland, hogbacks or related types of grave-monument have been found on the sites of Norse churches on St Ninian's Isle in Shetland, and on Papa Westray and at Skaill (Deerness) and Kirkwall in Orkney. These 12th-century churches were mostly small and simple in design, like **St Mary's Chapel** on Wyre, built close to **Cubbie Roo's Castle**, but some were more sophisticated. The quality of the masonry and details of design of the small church on the **Borough of Birsay** marks it as a special church, as befits the original seat of the earldom, while the church at **Orphir** stands alongside the home of a 12th-century earl and remains the only circular medieval church surviving in Scotland. The infamous murder on Egilsay of Earl Magnus Erlendsson gave rise both to the splendid cathedral of St Magnus in Kirkwall and to **St Mangus's Church** on Egilsay itself, a church graced by a tall round tower at its west end. This tower was formerly attributed to Irish influence, but it is now widely accepted as belonging, like the round church at **Orphir**, to a pool of ecclesiastical architectural fashions common to both sides of the North Sea.

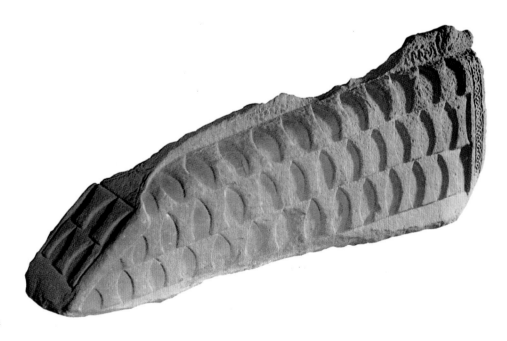

The hogback tombstone at **Meigle** (no 25). The snout of an elegant beast juts out slightly from the upper end of the ridge, and the roof-tiles are deeply cut with concave sides.

Orphir, Orkney. *Orkneyinga Saga* describes Earl Paul Hakonarson's stately residence in the 12th century. 'There was a great drinking-hall at Orphir, with a door in the south wall near the eastern gable. . . On the left as you came into the hall was a large stone slab, with a lot of big ale vats behind it and opposite the door was the living-room.' Part of the foundations of houses have been uncovered by excavation, but these are likely to date from later times. Traces of a horizontal water-mill of Norse date were found nearby.

The round church at **Orphir** may well have been built by Earl Paul, conforming to a European fashion in church architecture. Most of the nave was demolished when the later parish church was built (itself now demolished), but the semi-circular apse survives intact.

50

BY AD 900, the ethnic tapestry of Scotland was intricate and highly coloured. The confrontation between the Celtic tribes and the Roman army in AD 79 had been a purely military affair. Although the huge size of many Roman marching camps points to a Roman presence to be reckoned in tens of thousands, it is unlikely that many soldiers stayed behind when the army was withdrawn. In contrast, the invasions both of people and of new ideas during the subsequent eight centuries created a complicated mixture of Britons, Angles, Picts, Scots and Norsemen. More coloured threads were to come, with the Anglo-Norman penetration of Scotland in the 12th century and the contemporary but more restricted settlement of Flemish families in Lanarkshire, Fife and Moray. In no case was the actual number of newcomers very great but their influence was considerable.

The lasting influence of all these various invaders can be detected in language and placenames, literature, civil administration and other areas of historical documentation. The archaeologist can point to the evidence of imported pottery or coins, or to new ideas in buildings such as castles. For the 9th and 10th centuries, however, the most graphic embodiment of Scotland's mixed culture is in stone sculpture.

On the outskirts of Forres in Moray stands **Sueno's Stone**, a remarkable monument on several counts. At more than 6.5 m, this is Scotland's tallest surviving cross-slab. The style of its carving points to a fine mixture of Pictish, Irish and Northumbrian traditions, while interpretation of the great battle depicted on the back of the slab has led to many happy hours of argument. It was discovered in the early 18th century buried in the ground, and the fact that such a slender and long slab of

An elegant fowl on graveslab no 8 at **St Vigeans**.

sandstone survived intact suggests that it may have been buried deliberately for political reasons rather than having fallen. It is likely originally to have stood in or close to the spot where it was re-erected in 1726. The stone itself must have been quarried elsewhere, perhaps at Covesea on the Moray coast some 15 km away, and transported to Forres for carving; this implies a special reason for the erection of the cross-slab in this particular place.

The name, **Sueno's Stone**, was invented in the 18th century and has no bearing on the origin of the monument. Only the stone itself and its location can give any hint of why and when it was created and on whose orders.

Despite severe weathering at the top of the stone and a degree of overall blurring, it is possible to make out the sculptor's design. The cross occupies most of one face, the outline of its shaft and base infilled with interlace patterning, and more interlace decorating the background. Beneath the cross-base is a curious scene in which two figures, carved large to signify their importance, lean over a smaller or seated figure between them, while two small attendants wait in the background. The interlaced designs on each of the narrow sides of the slab have far more character than those on the

Opposite
Sueno's Stone, Moray: the tallest of all cross-slabs. The stone is now protected by a glass shelter. The scene beneath the foot of the cross may depict a royal inauguration.

cross-face; in particular, the upper part of the south side bears delightful spirals of foliage in which small human figures are perched. This type of design, the inhabited vine-scroll, was popular amongst Pictish sculptors, who borrowed the idea from Northumbrian art.

The back of the slab is entirely covered by a unique work of visual narrative. Divided into four unequal panels (the lowest panel being partly hidden by the plinth), the carving depicts densely-packed scenes of intense activity. Scholars agree that these scenes tell the story of some great battle, involving cavalry, foot soldiers and the beheading of the defeated – but who was defeated and who won?

The artistic style of **Sueno's Stone** suggests that it was carved in the 9th or 10th century by a Pictish sculptor possibly working for a Scottish patron, since the panels of figures are a device that became typical of Irish crosses in the 10th century. The battle could therefore have been between the Picts and the Scots, and a case has been argued for the stone having been set up by Kenneth mac Alpin to commemorate a series of battles and executions by which he and his Scottish forces vanquished the Picts in the mid-9th century. Towards the end of that century, Moray was subjected to intense attacks from Norsemen, and it is equally possible that the battle scenes on **Sueno's Stone** relate to struggles between the Norsemen and local Picto-Scottish forces. There is archaeological evidence for the destruction, sometime in the late 9th or early 10th century, of the great Pictish

fortress at **Burghead** on the Moray coast some 12 km from Forres, an event that was most probably connected with Viking attack.

But perhaps the neatest explanation of all relates to royal dynastic politics of the later 10th century. In 966, the Scottish king, Dubh, was killed at Forres by the men of Moray, in order that his cousin might become king, and, according to an early document, the body of the dead king lay beneath the bridge at Kinloss prior to burial. **Sueno's Stone** stands on the Kinloss side of Forres, and the curious arched object at the top of the third panel (reading the panels from the top of the stone downwards) can be interpreted as the bridge above a series of decapitated bodies, one of the heads specially framed to show its importance. Here then is King Dubh beneath the bridge at Kinloss, following his defeat at Forres.

There is no inscription on the stone to prove or disprove any of these theories – the observer must decide or keep an open mind!

Brechin is another excellent place to appreciate the blending of Pictish, Scottish, Irish, Northumbrian and even Scandinavian elements between about 800 and 1100. This was one of several early ecclesiastical centres in Pictland that had links both with Iona and with Northumbria in the 8th century, and at **Brechin** the links are visible in the surviving portion of an important cross-slab. In the centre of the Northumbrian type

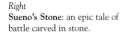

Right
Sueno's Stone: an epic tale of battle carved in stone.

Far Right
Sueno's Stone. In the top row, seven decapitated bodies, four figures carrying staves, and a pile of severed heads below something with a tapering profile, which has been interpreted as a stone tower or an ecclesiastical bell. In the middle row, the grim business of execution, and below, the massed forces of cavalry and infantry, the latter led by archers.

of cross-head is a rare carving of the Virgin and Child, a motif used by the Iona sculptors of the 8th century and probably derived from an illustration of the Book of Kells (or from whatever imported manuscript or object had inspired its painter). At **Brechin,** neither Virgin or Child has a halo, perhaps because of their curious headdresses, but both are encircled within a pelleted frame which echoes the pelleted halo round the Virgin's head in the Book of Kells. The literary background to this cross-slab is underlined by a Latin inscription, 'St Mary, the mother of Christ'. This slab was probably carved in the 9th century, somewhat later than the Pictish cross-slab from Aldbar, which is also displayed in the cathedral.

A decade or so after AD 1000, some important local figure commissioned an elaborate hogback tombstone (see p 47) in the Anglo-Scandinavian tradition of northern England but carved with decoration showing Irish taste.

By the late 11th century, **Brechin's** link with Ireland was strong enough to stimulate the building of a peculiarly Irish type of round tower; although now attached to the later medieval cathedral, the tower was originally free-standing. Its purpose was to act as a watch-tower and as a refuge in times of trouble, hence the single doorway more than 2 m above the ground, which could only be reached by a ladder which could be pulled up into the tower when necessary. Such towers were hideously vulnerable to fire, the wooden floors and ladders inside becoming fuel

The Virgin and Child cross-slab in Brechin Cathedral (Angus). The date of 1782 beside the angel, top left, was probably carved when the stone was found in a nearby garden. Sometime previously, the slab was trimmed to make an equal-armed cross, perhaps to decorate a building. The heads of the apostles, Peter and Paul, survive beneath the central medallion.

Sueno's Stone. While battle rages all around, decapitated bodies and severed heads lie below a canopy or a bridge.

Below
The superb hogback tombstone at Brechin is sculpted with foliage, animals and clerical figures holding books, croziers and a handbell; on the left, the end of the stone is carved into a massive animal-head, its snout unfortunately damaged.

53

The strategic advantages of **Dumbarton Rock** have been appreciated for many centuries.

within a chimney. One other such tower was built in Scotland at **Abernethy**, another ecclesiastical centre dating from Pictish times (see *Picts*). The doorway at **Brechin** is carved with a crucifix, clerical figures and animals, and is a rare early example of architectural sculpture still in its original position.

In a sense, these round towers were ecclesiastical fortifications, both built in places of considerable antiquity. In the secular world, it is difficult to estimate whether there was a hiatus between the fort-building activities of the Britons, Angles, Picts and Scots and the new era of castle-building that began in the 12th century, but it seems likely that some forts continued to be used when necessary even if none was built. There is certainly a marked continuity of site location, showing that in many cases the power-centres of early historic times became the power-centres of medieval times: the Scottish fort on Dunollie near Oban was replaced by a castle, as were the Pictish fort at **Urquhart Castle** near Inverness, the Anglian fort at Dunbar and the British fort on **Dumbarton Rock**. This pattern repeats one from earlier times, and it was clearly a means by which a new political power could be established. The Roman fort at Newstead near Melrose was built close to the native fort on

Eildon Hill North. On **Doon Hill** near Dunbar, the Anglian hall was built on top of a demolished British hall, and on the **Brough of Birsay** the Norsemen took over the site of an important Pictish settlement.

The typical 12th-century castle introduced by Anglo-Norman settlers was built of timber on a high mound known by the Norman word, 'motte'. The sites of more than 250 mottes are known in Scotland; many of the best preserved were the least successful, in the sense that they were abandoned rather than re-developed as stone castles. (See *Scottish Castles and Fortifications*.) Linked to this era of early castle-building and the development of a system of feudal landholding was the gradual establishment of ecclesiastical parishes. Many of the new Anglo-Norman settlers were encouraged to build churches on their lands (see another companion volume, *Scottish Medieval Churches*); and throughout Scotland, including the North and West, which were under the control of Norse earls, the 12th century saw a vigorous building of stone churches. During the same period, the first burghs were established, formally recognised towns with trading rights, and the prosperity and confidence of medieval Scotland grew apace.

Duffus Castle, Moray. The original buildings of wood that crowned the mound in the mid-12th century were replaced by a stone castle in the 14th and later centuries. This is one of several mottes in State care.

A typical 12th-century church, St Mary's at Crosskirk, near Thurso.

FURTHER READING

D J Breeze, *The Northern Frontiers of Roman Britain* (London 1982).

D J Breeze, *Roman Scotland* (London 1996).

D J Breeze and B Dobson, *Hadrian's Wall* (Harmondsworth 1987).

B E Crawford, *Scandinavian Scotland* (Leicester 1987).

A A M Duncan, *Scotland: The Making of the Kingdom* (Edinburgh 1975).

R Fawcett, *Scottish Medieval Churches* (Edinburgh 1985).

S M Foster, *Picts, Gaels and Scots* (London 1996).

W S Hanson and G S Maxwell, *Rome's North-West Frontier: The Antonine Wall* (Edinburgh 1988).

L J F Keppie, *Scotland's Roman Remains* (Edinburgh 1986).

G S Maxwell, *The Romans in Scotland* (Edinburgh 1989).

H Palsson and P Edwards (translators), *Orkneyinga Saga* (London 1978).

A Ritchie, *Scotland BC* (Edinburgh 1988).

A Ritchie, *Picts* (Edinburgh 1989).

A Ritchie, *Viking Scotland* (London 1993).

A P Smyth, *Warlords and Holy Men: Scotland AD 80-1000* (London 1984).

C Tabraham, *Scottish Castles and Fortifications* (Edinburgh 1986).

ACKNOWLEDGMENTS

Most of the photographs were taken specially for this book by David Henrie, Historic Scotland's Photographic Unit and the reconstruction drawings on pp 32, 44 were undertaken by Christina Unwin, to both of whom we are very grateful. We are also indebted to the following institutions and individuals for permission to reproduce photographs and drawings:

The Royal Commission on the Ancient and Historical Monuments of Scotland (pp 3, 23, 24, 26, 31, 39);

National Museums of Scotland, Edinburgh, courtesy of the Trustees of the National Museums of Scotland (Inside front cover, pages 1, 7, 9, 10, 12, 13, 15, 17);

Dundee Art Galleries and Museums (p 10);

The Hunterian Museum (pp 5, 7, 9);

Angus Lamb (pp 5, 11);

Peter Hill, The Whithorn Trust (p 35);

Michael Moore (pp 6, 7, 12, 13);

Graham Ritchie (pp 2, 19, 25, 44, 54).

HISTORIC SCOTLAND

Printed in Scotland from sustainable materials by Scotprint, Haddington.

INDEX OF PLACES MENTIONED IN THE TEXT

References to pages with illustrations are given in bold

Index to Map